VENUS RISING

VENUS RISING

HARRY WILLIAM DEAL

ORSINI
PRESS

Los Angeles, California
Austin, Texas

ORSINI
PRESS

Orsini Press
201 N. Carmelina Ave.
Los Angeles, CA 90049

Copyright © 2008 by Harry William Deal

──────── Publisher's Cataloging-in-Publication Data ────────

Deal, Harry William.
    Venus rising / by Harry William Deal.
    p. cm.
    LCCN 2007940128
    ISBN-13: 978-0-9797816-0-5
    ISBN-10: 0-9797816-0-4

    1. Deal, Harry William. 2. United States. Navy—Biography. 3. United States. Navy—History—World War, 1939-1945. 4. World War, 1939-1945—Personal narratives, American. 5. World War, 1939-1945—Naval operations, American. 6. World War, 1939-1945—Campaigns—Pacific Ocean. 7. Sailors—United States—Biography. I. Title.

D773.D43 2007   940.54'5973'092
                                           QBI07-600297

Designed by Peri Poloni-Gabriel, Knockout Design,
www.knockoutbooks.com

Printed in Canada
Printed on acid-free paper

FIRST EDITION

DEDICATION

To my lovely, patient wife, Yvonne,
Who blessed our home
With three wonderful children—
Beverly, Stephen, and Suzanne.

❋ ❋ ❋

CONTENTS

✳ ✳ ✳

ACKNOWLEDGEMENTS

✳ ✳ ✳

MY DEEPEST THANKS to my daughter Suzanne Deal Booth, who received the rough outlay of my WWII memoirs and edited and re-edited it to make the story more understandable. She nurtured the manuscript and guided the book along in every phase of the publishing. Without her help and enthusiasm, this book would never have been realized.

To Brookes Nohlgren, who so ably shepherded this book through the process of publication, and to all those who under her direction contributed their time and talents. To Steffen Foster for his dedicated efforts in every aspect of this project, and to Kathy Tillery Bouchard and Betty Jo Cozby for their help in locating old family photographs.

To the men and women of WWII who gave of themselves so freely to preserve freedom when the world was faced with totalitarianism.

INTRODUCTION

"A country with no regard for its past will do little worth remembering in the future."

—ABRAHAM LINCOLN

✳ ✳ ✳

THIS STORY CONCERNS ONE SHIP in a fleet of many during World War II. It is about one sailor on an ocean with many other men, struggling to stay alive and to win, at any cost, a war they did not start. This one sailor lost his diary at the war's end; so, nearly 64 years later I am compiling from memory a series of events and encounters with an enemy fleet.

The world as it is today is very different from what it was back in the 1940s. During WWII there was a clear enemy and a conclusive outcome. Since WWII, however, we as a nation have been involved in conflicts that have had no clear resolution, no winners or losers, just uneasy peace. This has been the case in various arenas of conflict—Korea, Vietnam, the Cold War, the Balkans, and particularly the Middle East. It is unfortunate that ongoing conflict will probably be with our young generation long after we of the World War II generation have passed on. Our hope for lasting world peace at the end of WWII did not really materialize as we thought it would, and the world now faces ongoing global conflict.

As a result of the 9/11 terrorist attacks in 2001, where we lost 3,300 Americans, our Commander-in-Chief—and about 250 million Americans—supported a reprisal against the Muslim extremists, who had been planning the attacks since 1996. Now, in 2007 as I write this book, after six years of war, we have not been victorious as planned, and yet we still must face the daily threat that this enemy is determined to wage a holy war against us.

This World War II adventure of the U.S. Third Pacific Fleet is mostly a true story, though some fiction may serve where memory has failed. Names of some crewmen have been changed, while ship names, encounters, and dates are fairly accurate to the best of my 86-year-old memory. Just know that my goal has been to tell it like it was.

My adventure with Venus, the second planet from the Sun, was a very brief and private affair. It was 1945, and I was west of Honshu, Japan's largest island, on board the U.S. destroyer *Trippe*. Our squadron of four destroyers was on bird dog patrol, seeking out downed pilots, dead or alive. One night when I was alone on starboard bridge watch, Venus made her very bright appearance in the eastern sky, revealing her eerie and other-worldly beauty. As this bright planet traveled across the heavens, I had a profound experience unlike any other in my life.

Chapter One

U.S. ATTACKED

✳ ✳ ✳

THE 1941 TEXAS TEENAGER was not all that different from today's teen. However, one factor gave young people of the '40s a different edge: we had endured, along with our parents, the worst depression ever to hit this country. It forced us to grow up learning to do without many things, and to get by with very little.

Throughout the Depression, cotton continued to be a major crop in the South. Because so much of the farmland had been overworked, the dustbowl was a reality. As with many other crops, no cotton planted meant there was no cotton to gin. During the Depression, my dad's workweek was cut to almost zero. Many weeks, he brought home a mere $9 paycheck. My dad ended up having a pretty steady job as head mechanic at the Continental Gin Company, the world's largest manufacturer of the saw and brush cotton gins—machines that separated the seed from the cotton. Still, everyone was on relief.

Going on relief was no disgrace. Once a month my sister, my dad, and I would pull our little red Radio Flyer wagon to the South Dallas fire station. We usually loaded the wagon up full with potatoes, flour, cornmeal, canned goods, sugar, and beans. Milk and bread were acquired at the local corner store. We had to make two loaves of bread and two quarts of milk last a week for our family of four. Then, in 1934 a new sister came along, making us a family of five.

Our home was on Carol Street in deep South Dallas. We were an affectionate family, and I was always called "brother" by my parents and sisters, Charlene and Betty Jo. I, in turn, called them "sister." We lived about two blocks north of T.G. Terry Elementary School and south of the State Fair of Texas. One day when I was about 12 or 13 years old, my buddies and I decided to scale the fair's south boundary fence to try to get in without paying. We simply had no money for admission. I was the last to start climbing. Shortly thereafter, a Texas Ranger happened by, caught me, and manacled me to the fence with his cuffs, where he left me until dark. When I finally returned home and explained what had happened, my dad reminded me that it cost only 10¢ to get in. But I still didn't have 10¢, so my older sister, Charlene, offered to loan me the money for the next time.

We also lived near the train tracks. This proximity to the railroad rendered a stream of hobos to our front door. Because my mother had been raised as an orphan in Ohio, she knew what it felt like to be hungry. Later when she was taken in and raised by her Great-Aunt Emma in Dallas, she was exposed to more affluence yet always felt that those with "more" should share with those with "less." For this reason, she kept a big pot of beans and a cast-iron frying pan of grits on the stove, plenty of biscuits and syrup, white oleo margarine, and a front porch with table and chairs to accommodate the less fortunate hobos. It was not uncommon for us kids to come home from school to find the porch full of ragged strangers being fed by my mother.

Many a day my father, my friends, and their fathers would band together and head to the woods and fields behind Wahoo Lake. Spread out 20 feet apart, armed with sticks and rocks and our dogs, we would return home with burlap bags full of rabbits. In those days, fried rabbit in bacon grease was as good as chicken. Between the lot of us we had only a few guns, and we could hardly afford the cost of ammunition. For example, a 20-gauge, black powder #6 Winchester shot (25 to a box) was 39¢—big money in 1934.

Every day, we 12- to 14-year-old guys would head out for crayfish and sun perch in the sloughs of Whiterock Creek. What a feast! My mother would fry up anything but carp. Mr.

Leatherwood, an old friend of my dad's, had planted a five-acre field of turnips. He had only harvested about half the field when an April freeze hit Dallas—and ruined his turnips. He offered up what remained of his turnips to his neighbors and my dad, as a help-yourself. We dug up enough turnips for a grand feast. The greens had frozen, but the bulbs were in pretty good shape. You would be surprised at how many tasty ways my mother could prepare turnips!

UPON LEAVING HIGH SCHOOL in June 1941, I enrolled in Aircraft Repair Mechanics Training, sponsored by North American Aviation, a California aircraft manufacturer that built the SNJ (Navy), ATG (Army), and Harvard ATP (for England). These craft were advanced trainers. A cadet would go through three stages of training: primary, basic, and advanced. North American Aviation later built the P-51 Mustang and B-24 Liberator heavy bombers between 1943 and 1945.

Anticipating trouble with the Japanese Empire's aggressive Far East campaigns, the U.S. military manufacturers were encouraged by the U.S. government to expand inland. Accordingly, North American Aviation chose a site on Mountain Creek Lake at Grand Prairie, Texas (between Dallas, Arlington, and Fort Worth), for their expansion location.

Since I had had some experience with sheet metal/welding and machine shops, plus two years of R.O.T.C., I decided to try the mechanics training program offered by North American Aviation. Accepted as a trainee, I went through six weeks of instruction in Dallas. I became proficient in the use of aircraft shears, aircraft aluminum, resistant welding, and aircraft riveting to military specifications, sub-assembly, and deburring.

In July 1941 I had just completed my training, for which I was paid 50¢ an hour—good money for the 1940s. One day a neighbor friend of mine, Ronnie, came running across the field, his excitement and shouting piquing my curiosity. Ronnie's explanation was brief and to the point. His parents had given him permission to join the Navy. Early in June we had discussed the service, and now he was ready. He said, "Let's join up on Monday!" I responded, "But I just completed my North American training course and I'm scheduled to report to the main plant at Grand Prairie on Monday."

Ronnie was 17; he would be 18 in August. I told him, "Go back and finish high school. Let's wait until next June when I'll be ready to join, too."

"I'm ready now! Bright and early Monday morning I will be at the Commerce Street recruiting station, with or without you."

"But Ronnie, they are going to pay me 55¢ an hour and give me four paid holidays a year, plus hospitalization coverage, and one week of vacation after only one year. When you turn 18, I can get you a job too!"

"No way! I'm quitting high school and joining Monday morning."

I realized that there was no talking him out of it. Off he went, across the field that joined his parents' farm to ours, his head full of future naval adventures. Ronnie did indeed join the Navy that Monday and was shipped to San Diego for six weeks of boot camp before being assigned to the USS *Oklahoma*. They sailed to Pearl Harbor for the Pacific Third Fleet operations.

I began work on Monday, August 1, 1941. My shift started at 5:00 PM and ended at 1:30 AM. My job at North American was very challenging. I punched out stainless steel firewalls on a table press. I was in charge of deburring wing ribs and spars, and later I ran a stationary uni-shear, trimming out stainless steel mufflers from the draw presses.

We soon went to a nine-hour day with a six-day week. Getting off work at 2:30 AM was no problem for us young guys. No curfew was in effect and, with all the Oak Cliff beer joints open until daybreak, we were set. We carpooled, usually six to a car. It was not long before I bought a 1935 Chevrolet Rumble Seat Coupe and carried two riders from South Dallas to Grand Prairie every day, a roundtrip journey of 30 miles.

✹ ✹ ✹

SUNDAY, DECEMBER 7, 1941, found me still in bed as my dad woke me with the radio blasting the terrible news. The Japanese had bombed Pearl Harbor and had sunk or damaged many of our first line battle fleet. Heavy damage was reported at the airfield and naval base. The news of ships sunk and casualties incurred kept coming over the radio.

The battleships *Oklahoma* and *Arizona* went down. The *California, Pennsylvania, Nevada, West Virginia, Maryland,* and *Arkansas* were damaged. Many destroyers were hit. No cruisers were mentioned. Our carriers—the *Saratoga, Hornet,* and *Lexington*—were at sea with some of the older battleships.

I received word from one of Ronnie's close school buddies that Ronnie died on the *Oklahoma*. He had been on duty when a Japanese armor-piercing bomb went down the stack killing all hands in the boiler room. He never knew what hit him. The *Oklahoma* turned over, and the *Arizona* went down with 1,100 men in the sleeping quarters—where they are, to this day, still entombed.

✻ ✻ ✻

Chapter Two

GETTING READY

✳ ✳ ✳

F ULLY AWAKE, I GRABBED A CUP OF COFFEE and
headed for our old hangout at West's Barber Shop. Most of
the old gang was there. We called our crowd "The Terry School
Twilights" and sometimes "The Deuce Alley Bunch" or the
"Second Avenue Losers." Since it was Sunday, all of the Second
Avenue beer joints were closed, so we sat on the benches outside
the barbershop and concluded that there would be a lot of dead
Japs when we were finished with them. Carl, Henry, Ed, and I
decided on the Navy, but agreed that we would wait until August
of 1942 to join. Gus, Don, the Huckabees (Dalton, Alton, and
Buck), and Ken opted for the Army. Ray, Bill, and Jessie chose
the Marines.

Returning to work on Monday, December 8, 1941, I found a
well-secured plant under guard. Our lunch boxes were checked

going into the plant and then checked again at the end of the shift. Within a few weeks, a naval air station was being constructed on the banks of Mountain Creek Lake. A primary naval cadet airbase was under way at Arlington, Texas. The area between Dallas and Fort Worth became a hub for aircraft manufacturing. Naval airbase training facilities along with Army air force training was taking place at Love Field, north of Dallas.

All of the South Dallas gang went about their usual routine. Job duties took up most of their time. We still got together occasionally, at which time we would do a lot of talking and Jap-threatening. A few in our South Dallas group joined right away as the "Pearl Harbor Avengers." The rest of our group bided our time, as we had non-Depression jobs paying non-Depression wages and we were needed on these jobs to aid in the war effort.

The North American Aviation Company encouraged all draft-age employees to stay on the job as vital defense workers. We were allowed a six-month deferment because the aircraft being produced were crucial to the war effort. Also, the California design engineers had completed the design of the B-24 Liberator bomber and had completed 90% of the design of the new super-high-speed, high-altitude P-51 Mustang fighter.

✻ ✻ ✻

EVEN SO, I KNEW I WOULD VOLUNTEER and when June 1942 arrived I informed Tommy Kildow, my North American Aviation supervisor, of my intention to join the Navy.

"Please hang on until you can train your Rosie-replacement. You'll need to train her on the uni-shear and all of the other equipment you use to perform your job. You'll also need to train her in spot welding," Tommy told me bluntly.

"Of course, Tommy," I said, shocked. I knew that no woman could ever do my job. Was I ever wrong!

One Monday night Tommy introduced me to my replacement. Mabel Hinkle was a 40-year-old mother of two girls, 10 and 12 years old. Her husband, Malcolm, was in the Dallas Army National Guard. Malcolm's guard infantry unit had already been shipped to North Africa. Mabel's mother was her "ace in the hole," as she cared for Mabel's two girls while Mabel worked the 5:00 PM to 2:30 AM shift. Mabel lived in East Dallas and carpooled with the other women living nearby.

That first night I gave Mabel a pair of special oil-proof gloves. She was grateful as she looked at the variety of nasty jobs ahead of her, but she was a tough cookie. She took to her responsibilities with grace. By the end of that first shift, through the work of all of the men and women in the plant, we had assembled the various parts of this aircraft. Our advanced training plane ended up as a flying wonder, which was ready now to receive the well-trained naval aviator who was capable of winning the war.

Feeling secure that Mabel had the skill and knowledge to perform my job after only one week of training, I could make my next move. I went to Tommy and told him about Mabel's amazing progress.

"She's incredible," I told him. "I truly was a non-believer until I saw her at work. She took to it like a duck to water."

"I know," Tommy agreed. "And I have four more lady recruits coming in next week. I'll have one worker on the firewalls, two deburring the rib spars, and one on the punch press. You know," he continued, "you still have your six-month deferment coming, and you could help with the training. I could give you a lead man's bonus of 5¢ per hour [raising me to 60¢]."

"I'm sorry, Tommy. I just can't. My buddies and I already agreed. The Navy needs us."

I left work early that morning, dropping my carpoolers off on Second Avenue. I ended up at my house around 4:30 AM, made a pot of coffee, and read *The Dallas Morning News* until my parents and young sister began stirring at 7:30 AM.

"Well," I announced. "Good morning. I just wanted to let you all know at the same time. I'm joining the Navy."

The reaction was not exactly what I expected. Although my parents were patriotic, they did not want to see their only son go into harm's way. My mother, in particular, was very anxious as her two brothers, Fred and Harry Skidmore, had served in World War I and had both been injured.

My parents said, "Take the deferment, son. Enjoy the money you are earning now. Maybe you and Laura [my occasional girl-friend] could get married."

I knew they were trying to save both themselves and me from the grief and separation of war. But, my mind was made up and they could tell I was determined to go.

It was the evening of Sunday, July 20, 1942, and the "Deuce Alley Bunch" sat down together to discuss our options; our war future was ahead of us. Ed, Don, Carl, our buddy Shaw, and I decided to enlist by August 1, 1942. Carl had a deferment com-ing from a small defense plant his brother owned, but like me, he declined it. Don was only 18 and had decided to stay with his dad for a few more months at the T&P roundhouse. The rest of us were ready.

Chapter Three

ROAD TRIP

✷ ✷ ✷

CARL AND I DECIDED TO TAKE A TRIP to Galveston since we were getting ready to join the Navy and had never seen the ocean before. Watching the ocean roll up on the beach in the movies was not like real life, so we thought getting a little salt water on us would make us real "Gobs," or seasoned saltwater sailors. Don decided to take a few days off and go along with us. Considering I was the only one with a car, they agreed to foot the gasoline bill. Regular leaded gasoline in the '30s and '40s was 15¢ to 17¢ per gallon.

It was a Saturday morning when I picked up Don on Metropolitan Avenue and Carl on Hamilton Street. All three of us crowded into the front seat of my '35 Rumble Seat. We tossed the duffle bags into the back and off we journeyed on Highway 75, which was the main highway from Dallas to Galveston. The drive was about 240 miles from Dallas. We agreed to rotate driving to stay on the road, stopping only for gas, restroom, and food.

Our first gas stop was in Corsicana, Texas. We were averaging about 20 miles per each 15¢ gallon. We munched on the peanut butter sandwiches my mother had made for us and kept moving.

To pass the time, we each began to tell a bit of our family history. I started the tales by recalling a story my father had told me about his father on the 1872 trip that had brought Grandfather and Grandmother Deal to Dallas. My grandfather, named William Allen Deal, and his wife made their way to Dallas from Yellow Creek, Ohio. Their journey started on a barge that moved downriver to New Orleans, after which they caught a schooner to Galveston. There they boarded the Houston and Texas Central train and traveled to Corsicana—the Deal family's first stop.

Grandfather Deal had a two-month stay in Corsicana ahead of him, as the tracks that would eventually lead from Corsicana to Dallas had not yet been laid. Finally, in October 1872, the tracks to Dallas were completed, and my grandparents made their way from there.

Grandfather Deal went to work as a cook at the Oriental Hotel in downtown Dallas. He eventually became maitre d' and retired in 1920. In 1925, while crossing the intersection between Commerce and Trunk, he was run over by a Buick Yellow Cab and was killed instantly. I was only three and a half years old at the time. I remember the day he died. He could not see very well and was on his way to the state fair when he stepped in front of the cab on Commerce Street. He was buried at Grove Hill Cemetery. Charlene, my sister, and I both stood to the side of the open grave and threw dirt on top of the coffin. My family had no money for a grave marker, so later in life my wife, Yvonne, and I had a stone quarried and transported to the grave.

Carl then followed up with a good story about his Italian ancestry. After arriving from Italy, his people settled in Mobile, Alabama, and pursued the fishing boat business. They ended up in Dallas in 1920, setting up a peanut business in South Dallas.

Don had his story too. His folks had come over to the Carolinas in the 1850s. His grandfather and great-grandfather had been railroad people. They eventually came to Texas in 1874, working on the Texas and Pacific Railroad. Don and his father continued what had become the family business of railroad mechanics at the Texas and Pacific Railroad, South Dallas "Round House."

By Sunday morning, we approached the Galveston Causeway and drove onto the seawall area. What a surprise! From the looks of Galveston, one would have thought the Japs and Germans were already ashore. The security was A-l. Galveston was no longer a vacation resort for wealthy Texans; it was an armed military bastion. The town was crawling with Navy, Army, and Coast Guard personnel. Jeeps full of shore patrolmen and MPs stopped us at every intersection. We explained our business, showing our driver's licenses, social security cards, and my "secret" clearance from North American Aviation at least a dozen times before one of the MPs finally pasted a "cleared" sticker on the windshield and we were free to go.

The search for a hotel was almost a lost cause. The Navy, Army, and Coast Guard occupied the Hotel Galvez, which had been recommended, as well as the other major hotels. Being requisitioned, most of the older hotels were occupied as well. The Houston Whorehouse syndicate had moved in: the older motels were quickly turned into places of entertainment.

Driving west on the seawall, we saw bunkers of heavy, large-bore guns in place. There were more under construction, all of them pointing out to sea. The Gulf of Mexico had its protection in a line of coastal guns with a range of six to twelve miles. Luckily, we finally found a third-class, seedy motel that was usually rented by the hour. We rented one unit with two rooms and two beds, a kitchen, and an upright icebox. The proprietor let us know that he had horses in the stables for rent and he seemed to be pushing this fact. Apparently, thanks to the "Ladies of the Evening," servicemen had little time for horses. After he had lit up his second Lucky Strike (non-filter in those days), I dubbed our new friend "Mr. Lucky Strike."

Don, Carl, and I found our room and were relieved to see that it did indeed have more than one bed. Carl and I were wound up with energy and thought a tour of the Strand might be interesting. The Strand was a seaport area that served as the main drag and was full of beer joints. Don, who'd been battling a cough for a few days, opted to stay in, thinking that cough syrup and a good rest would be better for him than cold beer and women. After prodding Mr. Lucky Strike for directions to the Strand, Carl and I were on our way.

The Wharf area was a beehive of good seafood, beer joints, and lots of servicemen. The joints were full of real sailors from the battleships *Texas* and *Arkansas*, as well as two cruisers and four destroyers. All of the sailors had one goal in mind while on shore: to spend their meager pay on the pursuit of happiness.

After a good seafood meal, we decided on the Dixie Bar and Grill, where most of the fleet sailors were hanging out. A little mingling around found us in the midst of the group from the USS *Texas*. By that time, those sailors were feeling no pain. Carl and I enjoyed a few rounds of Southern Select beer with our new buddies and became privy to some semi-classified information. Because of my "secret" clearance badge from North American Aviation and the fact that we were joining up once we returned home to Dallas, the sailors felt they could trust us.

It seems that all enlisted sailors, seamen, and rated petty officers had been on convoy duty, with two trips to Ireland thus far. They were now ordered into Galveston to add 40mm quads and 20mm anti-aircraft arms and report for duty in the Mediterranean. They told us all of this information and yet could not tell us their sailing date.

I had a long chat with a shipfitter first class petty officer. After listening closely to his shipboard duties, I was convinced that this was the rate to pursue. Carl had already decided that his rate would be boatswain mate, who was in charge of the deck crews.

Galveston was almost on blackout routines. So we finished our beer and our conversations and headed back to the hotel. The last few miles were without headlights.

Our plans were to head back to Dallas on Monday morning. Since there was a brewery in Galveston, we drove over to the Brewery Bar and bought a gallon of draft Jax Beer for $1.25 a bucket. The beer cost $1.00, the bucket was 25¢, and the three cups were free. So, there we were—three guys en route to Dallas through Houston, dipping beer from a bucket on the floorboard of a 1935 Chevy Rumble Seat Coupe. It couldn't get much better than that!

✾ ✾ ✾

Chapter Four

SOME TEXAS HISTORY

✳ ✳ ✳

As we were in an area where Texas history and Texas independence were born, we all agreed to take another route back to Dallas. Don was feeling much better after some aspirin, no booze, and ten hours of sleep. He suggested taking Highway 6 through Bryan/College Station because he had a cousin who had graduated from Texas A&M and he wanted to see "Aggie-Town." Coming into Houston on the 290 Highway west to Hempstead, we found an old town called Six Shooter Junction.

About three miles east of Six Shooter Junction is the famous Liendo Plantation, owned from 1873 to 1911 by Dr. Edmond Montgomery and his wife, Elizabeth Ney, a sculptress and one of the most colorful and influential women in early Texas history. It was in this house that Dr. Montgomery and Mrs. Ney used the fireplace to cremate their baby who had died of scarlet fever. Not wanting the disease to spread throughout the countryside, they had chosen cremation as the most sanitary means of disposal.

Earlier, in 1866, General Custer, his wife, and his troops of Michigan and Wisconsin Cavalry and Infantry had camped on the plantation. Custer's wife, Libby, traveled by wagon everywhere he was stationed. The troops had been sent to Texas after the Civil War ended. Being at Alexandria, Louisiana, they traveled thru the East Texas woods, thru Jasper, and on to Hempstead. The purpose of this visit was to be the occupation force overseeing that all slaves were freed according to the surrender terms. The Liendo Plantation had 100 slaves and 200 Yankee prisoners of war captured during the Battles of Galveston and Sabine Pass. In 1866 the Buffalo Bayou and Brazo Railroads ended at Hempstead. That same year Custer marched his troops to Brenham, where the local cowboys met the group and refused to let them into the town. Custer then marched his troops on into Austin, quartering them on the banks of Shoal Creek. His wife and brother were quartered on the University of Texas campus, in the building now called the Custer House.

We went on to Navasota, Texas, where Sieur de La Salle was murdered by his own men in 1689 while searching for a route to the north. Then we drove to College Station on Highway 6.

Touring this spacious campus was a must as A&M provided more officers to the U.S. Army during World War II than West Point did.

We moved on to Hearne, Texas, cutting off to Highway 39 to Mexia, then off on a blue highway to Tehuacana. This area of Texas was noted for an Indian battle in 1846 between the Cherokees, who migrated down from their reservation in Oklahoma, and the Tehuacana tribe. After wiping out the Tehuacana, the Cherokees returned to Oklahoma. The massacre was in response to the humiliation suffered by the Cherokees during the Trail of Tears—the forced march ordered by President Andrew Jackson of Cherokees out of Georgia and the Carolinas to the Oklahoma reservations that left half of the tribe decimated. The Tehuacana, on the other hand, had been allowed to keep their lands.

Don's people were of Cherokee blood. He had an extensive knowledge of Cherokee history and their bitterness toward Andrew Jackson for the unforgivable Trail of Tears. Why were we so up-to-date on Texas history? That's simple to explain: the study of Texas history was mandatory in elementary school and an elective in high schools in the 1940s.

Don suggested we cut off at Hearne and catch Highway 79 to Cleburne and view the clear fork of the Brazos' old reservation grounds. He had some background on the tribes who had lived there after being given the land by the U.S. Indian Agency as a hunting haven for remnants of the Tonkawa, Caddo, Waco, Cherokee, and Kickapoo tribes.

Chief Placido, a Tonkawa, was head chief of three of the tribes and considered a friend and ally of the Texas Rangers and in particular of the Agent Major Robert Neighbors. As the story goes:

> (Major) Neighbors alleged that the United States Army officers located at the neighboring posts of Fort Belknap and Camp Cooper failed to give adequate support to him and his resident agents. The unsympathetic attitude of the military aroused the hostility of many frontier civilians, who charged that the Indians of the reservations were committing depredations on the white settlements. In spite of threats of lawless characters to take his life, Neighbors never faltered in his determination to protect the Indians. With the aid of federal troops he managed to hold back the white people from the reservations, and in August 1859 he eventually succeeded in moving the Indians without loss of life to a new reservation in Indian Territory. On his return he stopped at the village of Fort Belknap. There on September 14, 1859, while he was engaged in conversation with another man, one Edward Cornett shot and killed him.[1]

---

1   *Handbook of Texas Online*, s.v. "," http://www.tsha.utexas.edu/handbook/online/articles/NN/fne8.html (accessed June 28, 2007).

It is said that when Major Robert Neighbors was forced to turn over the Tonkawas to the Indian agent in Oklahoma the old Chief Placido shed tears like a child. Major Neighbors wrote the same night to his wife in Texas.

I have this day crossed all the Indians out of the heathen land of Texas and am now out of the land of the Philistines.

If you want a full description of our Exodus… read the "Bible" where the children of Israel crossed the Red Sea. We have had about the same show, only our enemies did not follow us…

—MAJOR ROBERT S. NEIGHBORS, 1859

We breezed on through Cleburne to Dallas, planning to be at the recruiting station by 9:00 AM Tuesday. Carl and I were as ready as we were ever going to be.

Chapter Five

SIGNING UP

✳ ✳ ✳

CARL AND I MET at the recruiting station where other "Gobs-to-be" were already at tables filling out papers. Shaw and Ed, our old high school chums, were also joining up. Two younger boys, 17 years old, were sent home with papers for their parents to sign. Carl, Shaw, Ed, and I were 20—old enough to fight and get killed, no problem.

The forms had many medical questions. Answering the respiratory ones bothered me, as I had struggled with a critical asthma problem until about age 11 and I still battled hay fever every spring. I hadn't had an asthma attack for 10 years. When I was diagnosed with asthma at age 8, the doctor recommended that my mother take me to a more tropical climate and going west some 300 miles to San Antonio was suggested. My mother wasted no time. She used some inheritance money she received from Great-Aunt Emma to purchase a 1926 Chevrolet touring sedan, and away she took me and Sister Charlene to San Antonio. My father stayed in Dallas. Mama purchased a small restaurant; it was one of those food stands alongside the road, serving eggs, burgers, and southern cooking. It was located just across from San Jose Mission, built in 1718 by Franciscan friars. Though the mission was in need of restoration, the old walls were still standing and weekly services were held in the old chapel. Charlene and I felt that the mission grounds were our playground, and we were there all the time. We lived in San Antonio until 1932 when my asthma attacks ceased. Eventually, my father came to find us and we all traveled back to Dallas.

At the recruiting center, the older doctor looked at my medical forms, and then stuck a stethoscope back and front. He examined my ears, nose, throat, eyes, and feet. He even checked for a hernia. Being that I was 100% nude, he missed nothing!

After finishing at my feet, the old doc asked me, "Have you ever walked in your sleep, son?"

"No, sir," I answered plainly.

"Have you ever been prone to seasickness?"

"Not that I know of, sir."

The old doc looked me straight in the eye and stated, "Son, where you are going there will be no hay fever. Nothing grows on the ocean. The sands are wet and don't blow. And coconut trees do not produce pollen. If you walk in your sleep, your parents will receive a letter stating 'Lost at Sea.' I think you'll be fine."

I was thrilled when we all met together to recite the oath of allegiance. A second class petty officer informed us that we were in the U.S. Navy Reserves as volunteers for the duration of this war and six months. (Once the war ends, you have to be discharged from service within six months.) We were then routed to the basement of the Dallas Municipal Building, the same basement that would see Jack Ruby shoot and kill Lee Harvey Oswald in 1963. We were instructed to wait and a bus would pick us up for transporting. To where, I wondered? We didn't know.

Lolling around the basement, we finally saw a 1941 khaki-colored Chevrolet sedan come down the ramp.

A Navy captain climbed out and barked, "At ease. I am Captain J. J. Johnson, personnel director at the Grand Prairie Naval Air Station. You recruits will receive your boot camp training at the air station, as all other boot camps—San Diego, Chicago, and Washington—are full-up."

He continued hollering at us. "You men are instructed to go home, wherever that may be, and meet back here at noon, August 20th. When you report back, bring with you:

- 2 pairs comfortable walking shoes
- 4 pairs of shorts
- 4 white T-shirts

- 4 casual shirts
- 6 pairs old, good, white socks
- 4 pairs casual pants, blue jeans, or khakis

NO:

- hats or caps
- shaving gear
- toothpaste
- cigarettes

"We do have a few items at our new base. Uniforms and shoes and other gear have not yet arrived. The Red Cross has personal items for free. Your barracks are 95% complete; bedding and bunks are on base. The mess hall is now complete."

He kept going and we kept listening. "Two Marine sergeants will conduct boot camp training for a six-week period. These two Marines are the toughest sons of bitches you will ever meet. At the end of your six weeks, you will hate their guts."

All of us were surprised to find our Navy careers beginning just 20 miles from Dallas, some 300 miles from the nearest body of water—the Gulf of Mexico. The captain also informed us that we would be getting a paycheck of $54 per month from this date on.

Carl, Ed, Shaw, and I had a private meeting in the corner of the basement. We had just left jobs where we had been making much more and, now with our new income, all we could really afford to do with our whole week was to go jackrabbit hunting. So we made

a plan to meet at 6:30 AM two days later at Carl's house on the end
of Hamilton Street to head out on our little adventure.

✻ ✻ ✻

CARL AND I ROUNDED UP OWEN, who was already
classified as 4F because of a heart condition. His father owned a
1934 Ford V-8 dump truck, and Owen was always ready at any
time for a rabbit hunt, as long as we provided the gasoline.

We found two 16-gauge shotguns for Ed and Shaw. I had a
20-gauge bolt action, and Carl and Owen both had 12-gauges.
We ended up the next day at Levi's Deep Elm Pawn Shop, where
we purchased our Winchester black powder shells.

We took off on a Thursday morning for Plano, Texas, and
the rolling prairie lands. In 1942, Plano was only a cotton gin
town of 500 people. It had a water tower, a filling station, a
drugstore, a general mercantile store, and one grocery store. It
also had only one deputy sheriff, who had a Model A Ford sedan
as his squad car.

Owen had no intention of slowing down as he drove through
town, as he knew this stretch of U.S. Highway 75 was flat and
straight. We knew Owen's flathead 85-horsepower V-8 could
outrun the sheriff's hot-water Model A anytime. Sure enough,
as we passed the last small house at the end of town, the Model
A, in a blaze of black and blue smoke, came after us. He was hot

on our tail. There were the three of us in the back or dump bed of the truck and Owen and another pal in the cab.

From the dump bed I pounded on the cab top and hollered, "The Deputy's on our tail, Owen. He's smokin' at full speed."

Owen hollered back, "All of you lie down quick and hold on!"

He slapped that stick in fourth gear and away we went, leaving a trail of smoke behind us. Because we had encountered the Plano deputy before, Owen had his escape or "ditch" plan already between his ears. He had calculated when to start ditching the deputy, heading toward Frisco at about 65 MPH. At full speed, the deputy was going only 50 MPH. Owen cut off at the Santa Fe Railroad tracks going west toward Lewisville. He ran parallel to the track while the deputy kept up the chase for a few more miles. Losing ground and barely in our line of vision, the deputy gave up and finally turned around to head home.

I pounded on the cab top again. "Hey, he called it quits!"

Owen said, "Alright." He spun around and found a gate on the south side of the tracks. He crossed on the wagon road, opened the barred gate, and drove across the plain to a dry water gulch. Hiding the truck down in the gulch, we had found our hunting ground. Owen's father, a Dallas County judge, had permission to hunt this ranch, but probably would not have taken kindly to our outrunning the local law enforcement.

Spreading out across the prairie, quail, jackrabbits, a few rattlesnakes, doves, and hawks abounding, we smoked up the prairie. With every round, we would yell, "Got Tojo!" "Blasted Hirohito!" "Shot Namuari in the butt!" "Another round for Pearl Harbor!"

We eventually cleaned 30 jacks, 15 doves, and 20 quail. It was quite a haul for a three-hour turn. None of our game was ever wasted after a hunting trip. Our generation hunted for food; sport was always secondary.

Owen's father had made arrangements with James "D," who owned a barbecue house at the end of Spring Street in South Dallas. James was a very amicable black man whom we had all befriended over the years. James would de-fur the jacks he brought him and then sell the hides for profit to a glove company. His way of thanking us would be to barbecue all the meat in halves, furnishing us with Black Dallas and Grand Prize beer, and to have a big party. We filled his place to the brim. Blacks and whites alike had a ball.

Every evening before we left for boot camp, we would pile into my '35 Chevy and make the rounds to the It'll Do, Sprews, the Bounty, and the Taj Mahal ballrooms. It seemed longer than only a week, but at the end of it we all managed to meet, as instructed, at the police basement. Basic training was on our minds as we waited for further instructions.

Chapter Six

BASIC TRAINING

✻ ✻ ✻

SHORTLY AFTER NOON on August 20, 1942, a Navy bus pulled in, and two khaki-clad, mean-looking Marine sergeants rolled out. Cigars stuck out of the corners of their mouths. When they removed the cigars, stained teeth glared at us from the wide-open orifices. The lead sergeant reminded us of the well-known character actor Ernest Borgnine—big and stocky—while Number Two looked like a worn but still handsome Humphrey Bogart.

Number One barked his first command, "You sorry assholes line up in two rows, 17 to a row. Those that don't know how to count (holding up two hands), here's ten (leaving his right hand up), five more is 15, two fingers more is a total of 17. Face left and file onto the bus."

Number One continued to bellow, "I am Sergeant Hanes. My assistant is Sergeant Phillips. From this point on, in boot camp, we are 'YES, SIR, SERGEANT!'"

We headed for the Oak Cliff Viaduct and west to Arcadia Park through Grand Prairie and 15 miles to the naval air station. The conversation on the bus concerned the Number One sarge. Even though my pal Carl was short, only 5'8", he was so brawny I considered him a muscle-bound giant with arms the size of my leg. Carl was first-generation American, his parents were Italian, and he was naturally tough. At 150 pounds, he could bench-press 200 pounds with no problem and made it clear that possibly, after boot camp, he would meet Number One in town and rearrange his yellow front teeth. I guess he didn't like him very much.

The bus dropped half the load off at the newly constructed #1 barracks. A third class petty officer, the barracks quarter-master, told us to bring our clothes bags into the lower-floor office. The bus moved the other group into #2 barracks. The PO (petty officer) issued us two sheets, a pillow, and a blanket. The barracks accommodated approximately 150 men. Our group finished the occupancy of the first floor. In two weeks recruits coming in from Oklahoma, Kansas, and New Mexico would fill the top floor.

After a very short course on bunk-making, we were marched out and introduced to the new mess hall. We were instructed, "Take as much as you can eat, but eat all that you take."

This was our schedule:

> Morning Mess: 5:30 AM - 6:30 AM
> Parade Ground: 6:45 AM - 11:15 AM
> Noon Mess: 11:30 AM - 12:30 PM
> Parade Ground: 1:00 PM - 4:45 PM
> Evening Mess: 4:45 PM - 5:30 PM
> No liberty for eight weeks.

Boot camp training was all about work. And more work. We sweated and trampled dust in our street clothes and shoes. We washed and dried our clothes every two days. We ate three square meals a day but had no beer or recreation of any kind for six weeks. The captain had been right. We did develop hard feelings toward our drill sergeants. However, they were also on that drill field working with us every hour of every day.

At the end of eight weeks, our Number One and Number Two sergeants marched us all down to our base canteen, which had just been completed. They treated our two platoons to a stein of Schlitz and told us that we could have two days of "liberty" (aka freedom) that coming weekend.

I took my liberty in Dallas. It felt like a vacation, except that our being in uniform came as a surprise to some of our pals at our old recreation haunts. Our uniforms, underwear, shoes, fatigue dungarees, and sea bags were issued our last week in boot camp. The Navy woolen blues, caps, silk neckerchiefs, and white caps were comfortable but way too baggy. Most of us would end up at a Dallas tailor for alteration to our bell-bottoms and to make our shirts fit tighter. From that point on, everything we owned had to go into that sea bag, our traveling suitcase for the next four years. We were also issued canvas leghorns and pistol belts for the upcoming Navy Day Parade in Dallas in mid-November 1942. By then, the base would total 1,200 to 1,400 sailors.

THE BARRACKS WERE FILLING UP FAST. The parade grounds were kept busy and dusty with new recruits coming in from the overloaded boot camps. The Arlington Air Cadet barracks were filled with 350 Naval Aviation trainees.

This base would become a primary training facility. Two years of college qualified a man for Naval Aviation training. The aircraft used were Stearmans PT-6 Primary two-wing, fabric-covered yellow Perils. They were dubbed "coffins" by the aviation machinist mates on base, as well as by the cadets.

The two hangars for repair, salvage, and overhaul were completed and located on a quarter-mile-wide cement landing field between the North American Aviation plant and the naval airbase. I could look out of the barracks window and see the plant where I had worked just a few months before. I thought, "I sure have traveled far!"

Every day there were cadet training plane crashes in the corn and cotton fields around Arlington and Grand Prairie. Many young men and would-be pilots died while trying to fly these coffins. This took a heavy psychological toll on all of us.

Ed and Jim were assigned to the airplane repair and make-ready hangar, which was only about 100 yards north of our hangar. Carl and I were assigned to the airplane overhaul hangar, where our job was to take these bi-wing Stearmans, repair and salvage the wrecks, and keep as many planes as possible in the air. Cleaning the remains of a cadet pilot out of the cockpit and gathering useable plane parts to rebuild other planes was a very nasty and depressing job.

The SNJs (advanced Navy training planes fabricated at North American Aviation) were routed to our hangars for cleanup and test flying. It was expected that hangar repair personnel who had worked on aircraft as repairmen, overhaul, or make-ready had to accompany the test pilots at least six hours a month.

One of my first assignments was to accompany Lieutenant John Gabbert on his test flights. Gabbert was fresh off the aircraft carrier *Hornet*. He was a survivor of the Coral Sea battle and he was at our base on recuperating leave after having been wounded.

I'll never forget our first flight in a PT Stearman bi-wing trainer that I had just rigged up by resetting the wings with a tension meter. It was a two-seater, with my seat being directly behind the pilot. With my parachute strapped on and my seat belt fastened, I was ready to go.

We hit the runway at Ml throttle. Gabbert went straight up to 6,000 feet, dove down on a cornfield, and pulled up, leaving my stomach with the corn tassels. The lieutenant looked back at me, and I am sure I was as green as the cornfield below. He laughed his head off, evidently enjoying the situation. I was airsick the whole time we were in the air, and after what felt like hours of his cutting up, we finally landed. Then I had to clean up my own mess.

The next test flight was on an SNJ North American advanced trainer. This was a plane with which I was particularly familiar. The lieutenant went easy on me this time. We got up to 10,000 feet before he barked into the earphone, "I'm going to test the machine gun at Mountain Creek Lake."

There was a barge, painted white with a big red ball in the center. Gabbert dove down from 6,000 feet, the .30 caliber machine gun blazing away. He pulled out of the dive and looked back at me. I smiled; luckily no airsickness this time. He gave me the "OK" sign and made a perfect landing.

✻ ✻ ✻

Chapter Seven

BASE DUTY

✳ ✳ ✳

EVEN THOUGH IT WAS GRUESOME WORK we were doing, the base duty felt far from the war and we often joked that we were on vacation. One night in the barracks, we four—Carl, Ed, Shaw, and I—discussed our assignment. We decided that, after three months of this type of Navy life—though a full-time learning experience—it was not what we had dreamed of when we joined up to fight this war.

Every day of cadet training yielded crashes with injured or killed cadets. The enemy was 12,000 miles away and the causality rate for war preparation was far too heavy for our stomachs. I remember one time Carl and I were shaving in the barracks restroom. We heard the roar of engines and looked out the window. A Navy two-engine Boeing transport was landing with 15 sailors from Corpus Christi. The plane had made a bad landing approach.

The left wing tipped and dragged the runway. It bowled over and the plane exploded into a ball of fire. Bodies flew through the air like popcorn. The pilot, co-pilot, and 10 sailors died. Three others were seriously injured with severe burns.

It was about this same time that one of our best barrack buddies, Bill Davis, was killed on the highway while hitchhiking back to base. He had grown impatient waiting for the Navy bus at Arcadia Park and so he decided to hitch a ride back to the base and was hit by a pickup truck while walking along the highway. Incidents like this only heightened our building depression about not being a part of the real action.

During this time I also suffered an injury, though luckily it was not a severe one. It happened when I jumped off a wing while we had a Stearman in the pit for fairing, and I fractured my ankle. While I was in sickbay in a cast, there were six sailors in the "Clap Shack." Four had gonorrhea and two had syphilis. I noticed one sailor in there had his eyes bandaged. I asked the ward medic what happened and was told that the sailor had gonorrhea of the eyes.

I had two sisters and knew that, as a whole, Dallas girls were a good lot. They were decent and virtuous. What drifted into town when the sailors came was another story. Carl and I had steady girlfriends, Helen and Laura. We enjoyed dancing at White Rock Terrace and cajoling on Flag Pole Hill. We were not without sin ourselves, but we did follow the Navy's "Code of Sexual Conduct" very closely. We were told to use prophylactics and to choose our dates carefully. No question, the world is full of good-time girls who will lie down for a stick of gum, including the local barmaids who seemed to be full of patriotic passion. We were very careful.

While in sickbay in a leg cast, the grapevine gossip was that the base commander was assigning the sea duty. Carl dropped by and let me know that our request for sea duty had been honored. He, Ed, and Shaw were assigned to a fleet of oil tankers and were scheduled for completion by January 1943. They were to sail in early February to join the U.S. Third Fleet at Tulagi in the Solomon Islands.

Carl also told me that I was assigned to another ship and he advised me to call on Captain Larson to find out my assignment. Even though I was on crutches, I asked permission to go see Captain Larson, so the hospital doc, Lieutenant Jernigan, had a pharmacist mate drive me to the captain's office.

I arrived on crutches and the captain laughed as he commented, "Son, accident-prone sailors do not belong on a warship."

Looking at his detail roster, he told me, "You are assigned to the aircraft carrier *Enterprise*. It's now at Honolulu and due to sail by January. You should be shipshape by then. However, no one leaves this base until after the Navy Day Parade."

I asked, "Why are you assigning me to the *Enterprise*, sir? All of my buddies are going to New Orleans to board an oil tanker."

The captain answered but seemed puzzled, "Your records indicate that you attended Dallas Technical High School. You have studied foundry, welding, sheet metal, and machine shop, and have had automotive training as well. You also attended aircraft riveting school at North American Aviation and spent a year at their plant in Grand Prairie. Aren't you also striking for an aviation machinist's mate, petty officer rating?"

Even though I was very surprised at records being followed that closely during wartime, I answered, "Yes, sir, that is all true. However, we have a group of guys, four of us. We've been together since grade school. We joined the Navy as a group, went to boot camp together, and we've even had the same hangar assignments. We've taken every liberty together and feel that we should at least go to sea together."

Captain Larson seemed baffled by the schoolboy camaraderie and showing of brotherly bonding. He remarked, "The novel *Beau Geste*[2] addresses just this type of feeling. This is what I can do; I will give you a list of tanker assignees and if you find one of your equal rank and training who will trade places, I will make the transfer. As it stands now, the Navy can be flexible with your request."

---

2   *Beau Geste*, the 1924 adventure novel by P. C. Wren, was adapted to film several times.

I had six weeks to find a willing transferee. I put out word through my friends and it was only two days later when a seaman first class came by the base hospital. He let me know that he would gladly trade places. "The *Enterprise* carrier suits me just fine," he said, though his only experience in aircraft repair was as an engine overhaul and test technician. The next day, George Cuningham and I met in Captain Larson's office. The captain spoke his piece again about who would be crazy enough to trade duty on a "state of the art" aircraft carrier for duty on a tanker. He grimly reminded us of what we already knew about tankers: "One spark lands on a tanker full of oil and you're history." He told us both (again) to be ready for the Navy Day Parade in Dallas.

"After the parade, George goes to San Diego by plane and Harry goes to New Orleans by train," said the captain. George left immediately for San Diego to board the *Enterprise*. Later in the war when I learned that the *Enterprise* had been torpedoed at Midway, with heavy casualties, I prayed that George had not been one of them.[3]

---

3   The USS *Enterprise* turned out to be the most decorated ship of WWII, participating in all but two of the major actions of the Pacific War. Had I stayed with this assignment, I would have seen a lot more warfare, including downed planes, kamikaze attacks, and dying men, and I may not have survived. I don't know what happened to George, but I sure hope he lived a long and happy life. I have checked the casualty list available on-line and was glad to see that his name was not there with so many other brave souls.

My cast came off two weeks before the parade. I went back to work in the hangar. The petty officer assigned me Captain of the Head. He called it light duty and said I was to complete the duty until my ankle healed, which meant no limping. This job was keeping the restrooms clean and sanitary. The doc had me on daily physical therapy at the dispensary. My ankle healed fairly well with just a big knot on my anklebone.

While limping back to the hangar from the canteen one day, I noticed an officer coming my way. He was easily identified as Lieutenant Robert Taylor, on a naval base "Goodwill Tour." Robert Taylor was a well-known actor who was married to actress Barbara Stanwyck. I prepared my salute well ahead of time and we saluted each other in passing. He was a real good-looking guy.

Right behind him followed a big lieutenant, Wayne Morris. Morris was also a famous Hollywood actor who had starred in many westerns. He was on leave from the Pacific War and flying a Hellcat fighter plane. In passing, he too received my smart salute. Of course, I let my sisters know right away about my brush with fame. They drooled. My older sister, Charlene, was a South Dallas beauty who graduated from Forest High School in 1939. She later became a very successful saleswoman for Neiman Marcus in Dallas. At this time my younger sister, Betty Jo, was in elementary school. Both of my sisters were very serious

Hollywood movie buffs and big fans of the two good-looking actors who had smilingly returned my salute. They were mighty impressed with my encounter with celebrities.

Chapter Eight

ALGIERS NAVY BASE

✲ ✲ ✲

FINALLY THE DAY OF THE PARADE CAME. We
marched down Commerce Street saturating Dallas with
Navy blue. Our roster at this time was around 1,400 sailors and
cadets. We were well received by the citizens, and the crowd
cheered as we marched by. My parents were there, proud and
waving. After the parade, we were given liberty. We broke up
on Akard Street and immediately pulled off the leghorns. We
headed back uptown for treats and good Southern hospitality.
The Elks and Moose Clubs dispensed plenty of drinks and food
to those in uniform.

Carl, Ed, Shaw, and I caught the streetcar and headed for our
homes to bid our folks and girlfriends goodbye. It was December
1942 and we were finally off to war. We were very excited about
what lay ahead of us. With packed sea and duffel bags, we were

dropped off by our forlorn parents at Union Station on Monday morning. We boarded the Texas and New Orleans (T&NO) train and headed off to the land of Dixie. Twenty hours later, a Navy bus picked us up at the New Orleans Union Station. We crossed the Mississippi River on the Canal Street Ferry and headed to the Algiers Navy Base, which turned out to be a melting pot of the free-world armed services. We were curious and the Navy bus driver, a civilian, answered all our questions.

We asked him, "Why is there a French aircraft carrier docked here?"

He answered, "That carrier is the free French *Navies le Bern.* The French admiral in charge had fled Toulon months earlier to escape being sunk by British bombers and to prevent the French ships from falling into Nazi control."

He continued, "The French crew was not compatible with this decision. They proceeded to sabotage their carrier by running acid through the boiler tubes and through the gun barrels. There were no planes aboard the carrier when they left Toulon. The U.S. Navy is currently preparing to outfit this warship for active war duty. They have removed the unruly French crew to a nearby river barge and did not allow them to re-board their ship."

I asked, "What about those Russian ships? What are they doing here?"

He gave more information as we drove to the base. "The two Russian ships, a trawler and a gun boat, are being re-outfitted with U.S. 20mm cannons and U.S. diesels. They will join the Pacific Fleet when the crew has trained on using our weapons."

We also inquired, "And the Norwegian and Belgian ships?" As we arrived at the base, the driver said, "Well, boys, this is it. I don't know about those Belgian and Norwegian ships. But here's Algiers Navy Base. Welcome home."

Upon our arrival at the Algiers base, a chief petty officer met us. He assigned us to barracks #6. He also informed us that our ship was still in the Delta shipyard being converted from a Merchant Marine cargo ship to a Navy tanker. It would possibly be ready for boarding by January 15, 1943.

In the meantime, he said, "You boots will stand watches and attend gunnery school at Shell Beach and burn oil on water drills at the base pool." ("Boot" was the name for a sailor who had never been to sea.)

Noticing my limp, the officer told me to report to the base hospital the next day for an examination on my ankle. He then guided us to the mess hall and to barracks #6. The barracks quartermaster assigned us duties and said that the officer on duty (OD) would come by the next morning to assign base watch duties.

We were given a strict warning:

"DO NOT GO INTO NEW ORLEANS ALONE ON LIBERTY. AT LEAST TWO OR MORE BOOTS TOGETHER AT ALL TIMES."

The next morning we had mess at 6:30 AM, cleaned our second-floor barracks floors, scrubbed the heads, and made our beds. Carl, Shaw, and Ed were assigned dock duties and I was sent to the base hospital. I was told to soak my ankle with physical therapy treatments and report back to the OD for other duties. I had warehouse watch from noon to 6:00 PM. Liberty began at 6:30 PM.

Three of us decided on touring New Orleans. Ed stayed back on base and watched the evening movie. We three checked out of the south gate (curfew at the gate was 12:45 AM). We boarded the Navy buses, transported to the Algiers Ferry, and from there we were on our own. Finding a bar was no problem. All of the bars had their oyster menus, mostly raw with hot sauce and crackers. There were never any questions asked about our age when ordering booze. Many of the sailors were 18, 19, 20, or 21. The legal drinking age was 21, but no one seemed to care. There were even a few 17-year-old boys, but the New Orleans attitude was: *If you are old enough to die for your country, you are old enough to have a drink.*

We filled up on oysters and shrimp and found a party in progress at the Roosevelt Hotel. We ambled into the lobby, where we noticed that 95% of the revelers were officers and local belles. We didn't seem to be that welcome, so we wandered out and found a bar four blocks away. It was called the Freen and it was a real dive, but we liked it anyway.

We got on with our first New Orleans liberty and only left the Freen when we saw the "Frenchies" starting to filter in. Their attitude seemed to us to be anti-U.S., and with a snickering smile and his tongue out, one of them uttered something in French as we walked by. Carl, with enough Italian in him, remarked, "That crack was an insult to me, boys."

As we exited the bar, Carl said, "Wait outside. I'll be right back."

Seeing him wrap his handkerchief around his fist, Shaw and I knew what was going to happen. We followed him. The Frenchies had not yet sat down. The wisecracker had ambled to the bar. Carl walked up behind him and tapped him on the shoulder. The Frenchie turned around and suddenly a 5'8", 150-pound body was flying through the air. With a fist in the mouth, blood and teeth splattering onto the bar, the Frenchie fell like a rock. His buddies didn't make a move, but the bartender called the Shore Patrol.

We grabbed Carl and hustled him out. We hailed a cab and directed the cabbie to the Algiers Ferry. Back on base, we made tracks to the dispensary. The medic, an ensign doc, worked on Carl's fist and removed a piece of tooth from his knuckle. We had to make a report on the injury, so we told the doc exactly what happened—naturally, blaming the French sailors for starting it. The ensign doc's only remark was, "Good," and I guessed that these Frenchies had a petty bad reputation in these parts. He bandaged Carl's fist and sent us back to our barracks.

✳ ✳ ✳

ONCE WE GOT BACK, the quartermaster relieved us of barracks duty and instructed us to report to the officer on duty. The OD put Carl, Shaw, and me on additional warehouse watches. We were being reprimanded for our behavior. My watch at the main supply warehouse was from 4:00 PM to 8:00 PM, Carl's was 8:00 PM to midnight, and Shaw's was midnight to 4:00 AM. We were on seven days a week until further notice, with rotation of the four-hour watches per week. We sure hoped to be on our ship soon.

On my third day of 4:00 PM to 8:00 PM watch, while making the grounds tour around the warehouse, I passed a wooden eastside fence line. I heard children laughing. I peeked through a knothole in the fence and saw that they were playing lawn croquet. I also noticed an older blonde girl sitting on a bench. She was evidently supervising the younger kids.

The beauty of this girl was breathtaking. I felt I had to get acquainted with her. I wasn't really that bonded to Laura, my girl in Dallas. We had never discussed a long-term relationship and we agreed to date others as we pleased. I also told Laura not to grow old waiting for me because I was going to be somewhere in the Pacific for a long time.

I found a wide crack in the fence and yelled out, "Hello there, you on the bench! Could I talk to you? I am on guard duty and awaiting shipping orders."

To my surprise, she left the bench and walked over to the fence. I slid my pencil through the ¾-inch crack to let her know where I was standing. I stepped back so she could see that I was on guard duty. I had on clean dungarees, khaki leghorns, and a pistol belt with a 1911 Colt .45 dangling off the belt.

I told her, "My name is Harry W. Deal, Seaman First Class. I'm striking for a third class petty officer rating."

I stepped closer to the crack as she introduced herself, "I'm Francine Bolton. I live with my mother and two younger sisters here in base officer's quarters. My father is Lieutenant Commander George Bolton. He's captain of a heavy cruiser that's now in Norfolk, Virginia. He'll join us in about a week."

I informed Francine, "I am assigned to a ship being completed at the Delta shipyards, and it will be ready for boarding in a couple of weeks. We're scheduled to join the U.S. Third Fleet somewhere in the Solomon Sea. We will complete our shakedown cruise to Galveston and then to Corpus Christi for a cargo load of bunker oil. Then we transit the Panama Canal and join the fleet."

Since I was supposed to be on roaming guard patrol, timing was precious. I came right to the point, "Francine, my time is short here in New Orleans. Next week our crew is scheduled to go to gunnery school at Shell Beach, Louisiana. I am just a lonely Texan and would feel greatly honored if you would share a movie with me in New Orleans this Friday evening, my liberty day. *Gone with the Wind* is on at the Majestic."

She came to the point, too. "Dad would really prefer that I date officers. But my last date was with a lieutenant at the base officers' club and it was not very exciting. I found out he was married with two children in New Jersey, not a very good dancer, and could not hold his liquor. It yielded a rather dull evening."

She continued, "Mom feels that I am old enough to make my own decisions about who I date. I will let you know tomorrow since you are on watch until Thursday."

The next morning when I made my rounds at about 8:15 AM, she was waiting at the gap in the fence. Francine said, "I'll go to the movies with you next Friday, but my mother and younger sister have to come too."

I guess I surprised her by saying, "OK. The more the merrier."

We met at the Roosevelt Hotel. Her mother was a real Tennessee beauty with a beautiful name, Grace. Her younger sister, Joanne, maybe 13 to 14 years old, was a beauty in the making. The mother and daughters had seen *Gone with the Wind* twice already and I had seen it once in Dallas.

I made the point of sitting beside Francine and we all enjoyed the classic once again. Then we all walked down the street to Offal's Oyster Bar and had a feast of shrimp, crayfish, and gumbo.

After dinner we walked down to the Algiers Ferry. They decided to catch a taxi to the base and I was going to stay in New Orleans to meet up with my buddies. As Francine had on a light sweater, I removed my Navy pea coat and slipped it around her shoulders. In the process of the coat transfer, I kissed her good evening. Mrs. Bolton smiled and Joanne giggled. I told Francine I would see her at the fence line when I returned from Shell Beach.

I met up with my buddies at a Bourbon Street pool hall, and when I told them about the movie date with a lieutenant commander's wife and two daughters they could not believe it. The guys kidded me all night about my so-called "ice cream date" not only with a Navy commander's daughter, but the whole family!

✳ ✳ ✳

Chapter Nine

GUNNERY TRAINING

✳ ✳ ✳

SATURDAY MORNING WE BOARDED A BUS for a one-week stint of gunnery training at Shell Beach, Louisiana. We crossed over 30 miles of shell roads and salt flats. Millions of mosquitoes as large as butterflies attacked us. The bus driver warned us to stay out of the swamps, saying, "Louisiana alligators are as large as tanks and they just love Texans for dessert!"

The gunnery base consisted of two barracks, a mess hall, the base crew's quarters, a baseball diamond, and a long firing range with 20mm AAs and 40mm Bofors (both were types of anti-aircraft guns) and a line of three-inch .50 caliber deck guns. Our crew numbered about 20 at this time and there were 70 more sailors from other ships. Barracks #2 was loaded with Russian, French, and British sailors whose ships were being outfitted with U.S. guns. Our barracks (#1) was a two-story, quickly built wartime bunkhouse equipped with board beds, no mattresses. The Cajun cooking they provided was really great, and overall we really enjoyed this part of our training.

The first day, we had classroom work where we learned the functions of the new Sperry 20mm auto-loading gun sight. The unit would pick up the target and set for the normal 20mm range. When the target was picked up, the unit automatically allowed for the speed of bullet lead-time. Like the Sperry-Rand bomb sight in use on all B-17 superfortresses, these were very innovative procedures. However, when in battle and under fire, you tended to ignore the sight frame and follow your tracers to your target—every fifth to seventh shell was a tracer.

The next four days were spent on the firing range with the 20mm and three-inch .50 caliber deck guns. We didn't receive training on the 40mm "pom-poms," as our ship would not be outfitted with these. We would have a five-inch .38 caliber deck gun on our stern mount, but that training was not available.

The Russian sailors were "gung ho" on the 20mm guns. They would not use the Sperry sight. They sighted along the barrel and one day they nearly shot down the BT-19 (a basic training plane with a 400 Pratt Whitney engine made by Douglas Aircraft) target-towing plane. The pilot dropped by the base commander to complain about the closeness of shellfire to his tail. The base lieutenant explained to him that the "Ruskies" were guilty and would be watched closely. The pilot was surprised, though, as he thought it was the dumb Frenchies who had purposely tagged him too closely. I guess they were being blamed for everything that went wrong.

The British sailors were very proficient and attentive, but the Frenchies, or "Frogs" as the British called them, were not interested in war games. This group only wanted the chow hall and booze when they could find it. Carl looked the Frenchies over, checking for one with two front teeth missing. He wanted to finish his dental work on what was left, I think. Lucky for Carl's Frenchie, he was not with this group.

The Russians were an interesting lot. We had a lot of fun trying to teach them how to play baseball. The batter would stand on the plate and hold the bat in front of him and chop at the ball. When they ran the bases, you had better move over or you would be trampled into the dirt. The Russian pitcher would throw as hard as he could at the batter. He thought that if he maimed the batter then the game would be over. At chow time, we learned that the Russians had never been exposed to tomato ketchup before and that they loved it. They put it in their coffee, in their cereal, on bread like butter, and eventually they rid the tables of extra bottles so that they could slurp on the stuff in their barracks at night.

❋ ❋ ❋

RETURNING TO THE ALGIERS BASE, we were informed by the base OD that our ship would be delivered by the shipyard pilot the following week. It would tie up at the Rice Mill docks at New Orleans. We had two days of shore liberty left before boarding. The OD also told me that Commander Bolton's family had been moved to Norfolk, Virginia. His cruiser had been assigned to the Atlantic Fifth Fleet. So be it, I decided. No more movie dates with the lovely Francine.

Ed, however, somehow managed to round up four New Orleans belles for a Saturday night dance at the Fireman's Ball. It was to be held at Marrero, on the Algiers side of the river. Ed, Shaw, Carl, I, and a few more of the Algiers barracks crew hauled off on the Marrero local bus up Highway 18 for the Fireman's Ball.

While on the way, I asked, "Hey, Ed, where did you happen to meet these Louisiana belles?"

He stated, "I was on a tour of the Delta shipyards with the Signalman's School. One of the girl welders invited me to the Fireman's Ball. I told her I would only agree if she could round up three more dates for my friends."

Ed was grinning as he told the story of the dating coup. It seemed a personal triumph for him. We were happy to oblige and met our dates by the flagpole as agreed. Ed introduced us to our dates and paired us up on the spot.

My date was Laverne Broussard, a tall, big-chested Cajun beauty. Carl's date was shorter, but a well-stacked Italian girl named Marie. Shaw's date was a 6'0" well-proportioned girl whose name was Greta. Ed was with the lovely Creole prize, Melba de Grasse.

To enter the Fireman's Ball, we had to make a donation at the door. Inside we found a large, round table, where we were offered endless bottles of Falstaff beer. The Cajun food was piled on a long table at the back end of the dance floor. A paper plate was issued to each of us and ample helpings began. There was fried crayfish tails, boiled shrimp, Cajun rice with Creole sauce, fritters, and garlic-toasted French bread. There were small bowls of gumbo to round it all off. Second helpings were encouraged and, for the servicemen, all the beer was on the house.

After we ate, the tables were removed and the band appeared and started setting up their speakers and bandstand. They unfolded two guitarists, two fiddlers, a drummer, a cymbalist, two accordionists, a mouth harpist, and two lovely Creole vocalists. The first piece was "San Antonio Rose" played in full Cajun fashion. I would bet that the sound moved up the river as far as Baton Rouge, some 100 miles away.

Everyone was dancing together. There were little boys and girls, big boys and girls, and old folks—these Louisianans sure knew how to have fun! There were no wallflowers at this ball and no fights either. There was just good ole Bayou Country dancing. Our girls knew everybody, and after the fourth number, dancing partners were up for grabs. We were all having big fun on the Bayou.

After three hours of exhausting dancing, we decided to catch a local bus, cross the river at the ferry, and visit a few lounges before curfew. The girls let us know that they didn't need to be home until 1:00 AM. Their husbands worked at the Delta shipyards and didn't get off until 1:30 AM. They only had to have time to send their babysitters home and fix a quick snack for the men folk. This was the first we had heard about husbands and kids. The shock was short-lived, though. We were all having fun, which evidently was the New Orleans way of life.

Around midnight we found a lively lounge on St. Charles Avenue and dropped in for bourbon on the rocks and a platter of oysters on the half-shell complete with crackers and Creole sauce.

The bar was a 25-foot-long, high-stool affair. It was filled with sailors and soldiers. There was a hefty, big-chested blonde on the far end. Our table was facing the bar's backside. About 18 pairs of eyes peeled right toward the blonde. The blonde decided it was time for a showdown. She unbuttoned her blouse and pulled out a very large and pearly-white breast, which she promptly flopped on the bar. All eyes rolled to the right. The blonde stared to the left and yelled, "Alright, all you bastards, take a good, good look!" And boy did they! Our girls had a huge laugh and shouted, "Bravo! Bravo!" As she buttoned up, everyone clapped. The blonde became a star and was showered with drinks and shrimp cocktails for the remainder of the evening.

As the oysters disappeared, we decided to walk the girls to the Algiers Ferry and say goodnight. As we moved along, though, two of the girls called out, "Potty time!" As all of the stores and shops were closed, the girls stopped at the opening vestibule of some store and did their business in private. We just kept on moving, laughing, and having fun until we got to the ferry. We kissed the girls goodnight and got them on their bus home.

As we journeyed back to the barracks, we all jokingly reminded Ed about the caliber of dates he had managed to round up. "In the future, Ed," we teased him, "try a little harder to find single girls for our blind dates!"

He replied, "Don't worry. These are our last dates for a long time. The next fraternizing with girls won't be until we hit Balboa, Panama, and then we will be lucky to meet girls who can speak English."

Evidently, Ed had the straight story from the shipyard. We were to board our ship in a few days. We would hit the Panama Canal by late February 1943.

✳ ✳ ✳

Chapter Ten

ON BOARD

✳ ✳ ✳

S UNDAY MORNING the base officer on deck came by
our barracks and reminded us to pack our sea bags, have
an early breakfast, and be at the Algiers base dock at 7:45 AM. A
Navy launch would transport us to the ship, which was about a
mile upriver at the Uncle Ben's Rice docks.

There were 10 on the crew of the USS *Raccoon* in our
barracks and about the same number from the other barracks.
When we spotted the big, iron monster—our new home—it
was quite a thrill. It was a light Merchant Marine gray color and
had workmen still swarming all over it, installing the degauss-
ing system inside the gunnels and around the entire ship. The
large DC generator was underneath the five-inch .38 caliber gun
mounts and, when activated, this system would demagnetize the
entire hull.

We were dropped off at the dock and marched up the gangway. Saluting the flag, we lined up on the forward deck for further orders. All officers had boarded the day before, and most petty officers three days prior to that. The captain was Lieutenant Molinard. He introduced the executive officer, Lieutenant Junior Grade Hal Morley; the communications officer, Lieutenant Junior Grade John Copeland; and the deck officer, Lieutenant Junior Grade Jorge. Then he followed up by introducing all the petty officers and warrant officers. He briefly detailed their duties.

The captain explained that the ship would be commissioned that week, as soon as all the crew members reported on board. Then we would sail up the river to the ordinance docks and load up on ammunitions. We would take on three-inch .50 caliber, five-inch .38 caliber, 20mm, and for small arms: rifles, shotguns, and .45 caliber 1911 semi-automatic pistols. In closing, the captain informed all hands that we would muster at 6:30 AM on the aft portside deck every morning until further notice. The only personnel excused would be those on watch or on specific duties.

The first class boatswain mate called the names that would be on his deck crew and stated that their bunkroom would be under the aft five-inch .38 gun mount. I was assigned shipfitter, which I had already professed my desire to do through our base officer on deck. Carl was given deck crew, and Ed was signalman. Our bunks were assigned according to the location of the area of the ship we were to serve. Shipfitters would take loading and discharging cargo fuel. The fuel and our bunkroom were located forward in the main house next to the pump room. The mess hall and galley was amidship and all hands were quartered in the house except the gunner's mates and deck crew.

Our shakedown cruise would be up and down the Mississippi River. We would take on ballast and continue test cruises in the Gulf. Our last remnants of crew boarding took place and our total compliment of 74 enlisted men, four officers, and one warrant officer was complete.

We set steam, unleashed our hawser lines, and lowered the Navy Jack, which was all blue with 48 stars on the bow. We steamed up the Mississippi into Westwego and Marrero for ammo and further food supplies and then went downriver to the Gulf of Mexico. By this time, it was 10 days since boarding. We became well acquainted with all crewmembers. About half of the crew was from the Southern states, mostly volunteers. The other half of the group, from above the Mason-Dixon Line, had been drafted. There were three officers from the East Coast and one from Mississippi. Our warrant officer was from Jamaica. The head steward for the officer's mess and the three stewards mates (all black men) were considered the luckiest on board. They had bunkrooms on the 2nd deck and ate food from the officer's mess, which was the very best on board. They had no deck watches but were trained and assigned to the aft 20mm AAs.

Steaming into the Gulf of Mexico, we bypassed Galveston Island, even though we were supposed to take on fresh beef there. We went straight on to Corpus Christi for the cargo oil and meat supplies. Our sister ship, the *Porcupine*, had sailed two weeks ahead of us with a cargo of 100-octane aviation fuel. We met a few of their crew and found out that the *Porcupine*, like the *Raccoon*, was a former Merchant Marine ship converted from cargo to fuel tanker to serve the Third Fleet in the Pacific.

We arrived in the Corpus Christi ship channel, and a port pilot came on board to guide us through the channel, under the drawbridge, and into the tank storage and fuel loading docks. Our ship was approximately 500 feet long and 68 feet wide, with a load draft of 29 feet. That meant that, when it was fully loaded, 29 feet of our ship would be underwater, leaving six to seven feet freeboard. After tying up at the oil dock, we took on two six-inch fuel hoses both fore and aft, lined up our tanks, and began to load black cargo oil into the cargo tanks. Keeping the ship trim was very important and our captain made it clear that he would not tolerate more than a five-degree list. For 15 hours, we manned tank valves on three forward and two aft tanks, finally topping off at approximately 12,000 barrels of black, slightly refined cargo oil. We were to deliver this oil to the Third Fleet somewhere in the Solomon Sea, about 11,000 miles from where we were then docked.

There was no time for liberty in Corpus. We loaded on coffee, sugar, more meat, tons of canned goods, tins of cornmeal, and kegs of flour. The next morning, a tugboat tied on and we tired boys were ready for a long sea voyage. While being maneuvered toward the deep ship channel, we floundered in the mud. Our 10-ton screw was churning up mud, so more tugboats were called in. We finally moved into the deep channel and headed for the open sea. As we neared the raised drawbridge, we were all mustered on deck in our white uniforms and waved goodbye to the Corpus Christi belles who had come out to cheer us. We were finally heading out to Balboa, a part of Panama City, in the Panama Canal Zone.

The trip to Panama was quiet and uneventful. We had no air escort until we hit the Yucatán Peninsula. As there had been "U-boat" warnings issued by the Galveston Navy command, we had to be ready and stand gun watch every morning from 6:00 to 9:00 AM. One bright day, after duties were over, Shaw, Carl, and I were sunning on the aft five-inch gun deck when out of the blue came a roaring noise and we saw this enormous blimp coming toward us. We almost fell overboard, shocked by the size and noise of this big monster coming down at us in the middle of the Caribbean Sea. Turns out, this was our air escort!

✳ ✳ ✳

Chapter Eleven

ADJUSTING TO SEA LIFE

✳ ✳ ✳

UPON OUR ARRIVAL AT BALBOA, the OD informed us at muster that we could have liberty. We were told to stay in dress white uniforms until midnight. We had our rules—no liquor allowed on board. The Navy set up prophylactic stations at the entrance to all "Boys Town" areas, and you were not allowed to exit unless treated for venereal diseases.

The freshwater distilling system on board produced enough freshwater to enable our entire crew to have at least one shower per week. We spruced ourselves up and dressed in our Navy whites. A small group of the Texas and Georgia boys decided on the Blue Moon Night Club, which was remotely located outside of Balboa. We hailed a taxi, and the driver already knew the way.

The six of us were a long way from home and sauntered into the Blue Moon with some attitude. The maitre d' asked us if we would like girls to dance with or whatever. Our response to this helpful man was unanimous. With one snap of his fingers, six lovely ladies descended the staircase as we sat down. Most of them were very young, 15 to 16 years old, girls from the neighboring provinces. I chose to be with an older girl, about 25, who though plump was quite a sight.

The drinks arrived quickly. There was fake champagne for the girls and bourbon on the rocks for the guys. After three hours of dancing and drinking, we all retired to a suite of lavishly decorated rooms at the top of the stairs. This old place looked as though it had probably been a governmental palace at one time.

The evening turned out to be quite expensive, and with our average monthly pay rate of $66, the final bill nearly wiped out our combined Navy pay. We returned to the dock entrance and the Navy corpsmen were waiting at the prophylactic station. When they got through with the treatment process, the general feeling among the boys was, *it was not worth it*. We'd learned a hard lesson.

Some of the sailors decided to smuggle in a few bottles of Old Fitzgerald booze strapped to their legs under their trousers. As we found out later, this was a mistake. The awaiting shore patrolmen had their methods of detecting hidden booze. As the sailors came into the dock entrance, the patrolmen would use their heavy nightsticks to hit sailors' legs where booze was normally hidden, causing many a sailor to board the ship with bloody legs.

Life on board wasn't without its share of adventures. Our first class fitter found a slight oil leak coming from underneath our ship. He felt it was coming from the main sea valve and possibly from the #3 main cargo tank and was leaking about a barrel every 30 days. The captain decided we would sail out to the Solomon Sea and have the repairs made at Espiritu Santo's naval repair station, some 33 days or 6,500 miles from Panama. We set steam and cast off on March 10, 1943. We went through the locks into Gatun Inner Lake—an extraordinary experience.

While we were looking over the bow going into the inner lake, a large snake—about 24 inches in diameter and 20 feet long—was coming at the port side. It dove deep, apparently to go under the ship. I yelled at La Rue, a third class gunner's mate, on the other side to watch for it, but no snake came out the other side! I ran to the stern to see if it had been ground up in our big screw. No! The sea monster was swimming toward the jungle. Evidently, going under large ships was no problem for it.

We had taken on a passenger—a pilot—and we dropped him at San Cristobal on the Pacific side of the Panama Canal and began our 6,500-mile journey to the Solomon Sea. Our ship, being a converted merchant vessel, had dummy cargo booms and house amidships. It looked like a dry cargo ship, only in our holds we carried 12,000 barrels of bulk fuel oil that was destined for the U.S. Pacific Third Fleet. As I mentioned, our sister ship, the *Porcupine*, was about 12 days ahead of us and was destined to join the U.S. Seventh Fleet at New Caledonia.

Our top speed of 12 knots was a hindrance to our safety and we would be dead meat for the Japanese "I" class submarines, which were the largest in the world. They carried torpedoes as big as the snake I had seen—with tubes that were 24 inches in diameter and 20 feet long, and loaded with armor-piercing warheads. These were called "Long Lance" torpedoes.

The Japanese submarine commanders had a kill priority list, which was common knowledge to the U.S. Navy. It went in this order:

1. U.S. aircraft carriers

2. U.S. fleet tankers

3. U.S. cruisers or destroyers

4. U.S. APA-AKA troop ships (armed attack troop and cargo carriers)

5. U.S. large LST (landing ship tank) landing ships

U.S. battleships were usually at a lower priority because of the heavy screening provided by cruisers and destroyers. We lost only two battleships during the entire Pacific campaign, the USS *Arizona* and the USS *Oklahoma*. Many battleships were damaged by the Japanese kamikazes (meaning "divine wind") but survived to fight on.

As we moved across the southern Pacific waters, air patrols from San Cristobal covered us for the first 1,000 miles. After that, our consistent gun watches covered our 12 knots per hour. During this crossing, we saw two U.S. submarines and four cargo ships (AKAs) moving east toward the canal, but for 15 days there was not even a gooney bird in sight.

Most of the crew, including the Texas boys, had never seen so much water even though 75% of Earth is covered by the stuff. As we neared the huge Navy repair station at Espiritu Santo, south of the Solomon Sea, a British destroyer had to escort us in. Our captain had wired in by code about our predicament of a slow cargo oil loss and we were immediately escorted to a repair ship—a floating manufacturing vessel loaded with vertical mills, engine lathes, Heliarc welders, resistance welders, foundry, and every tool imaginable as well as highly skilled craftsmen in every field.

We anchored about 60 feet off the repair ship starboard side and a Navy tugboat tied onto our stern to help align us in position. A barge came alongside; sailors came aboard with a six-foot-wide, heavy roll of treated canvas sewed with a double seam with approximately 30 grommets. While Navy divers jumped into the water holding one end of the canvas, our crew held the grommeted end to the ship's center on top of oil cargo hold #3.

The divers went under the ship with one-inch rope coming out the other side. They climbed up "Jacob's Ladders" and we all began to pull the canvas. There were about 20 sailors who held the grommeted end while 20 more pulled the raw end to the center of the deck.

The repair crew took charge of this giant Band-Aid, cutting the canvas neatly and making three folds. They riveted the folds together and applied 30 equal grommets about a foot between the canvas ends. A diver dove back under the ship to align the giant Band-Aid over the main sea valve. Then they began to lace the two ends together like a shoe. After it was fully tightened, our shipfitters crew descended to the bottom of the pump room and began to disassemble the main valve. Our initial diagnosis of our damage had been very accurate, as we found a chunk of oak barrel stave jammed into the ball valve. It was just enough to allow a slow leak. The canvas Band-Aid held the sea pressure at bay while we completed the clean-out and reinstalled the valve. When the canvas was removed, the valve held.

The captain came on deck, thanking and praising the repair crew for the speedy repair. He also passed the word that we would be steaming for Noumea, New Caledonia, in the South Pacific, which was a fleet and transport staging area. Then we would rendezvous at Efate in the French New Hebrides islands, northeast of Guadalcanal.

While we were steaming toward our new destination, the Japs retired the "Tokyo Express"—the Allied name for Japan's Imperial Navy ships that would deliver personnel, supplies, and equipment to Japanese forces at night in and around New Guinea and the Solomon Islands—to their secure base in the Philippines and Formosa. They moved their Imperial Marines to New Britain, Bougainville, and both the Marshall and Gilbert Islands. Meanwhile, there were also Imperial Marine and Naval buildups at Iwo Jima and Chichi-jima.

Arriving at Noumea, we saw a beehive of activity. The Solomon Islands were secured in blood and water amid the bodies of many young men, all of whom died in their prime for this piece of land. The first sight to greet us was a very large vessel underwater with its masts sticking up. The vessel—the USS *President Polk*—was a liner converted to a troop transport and loaded with 2,000 Tenth Army troops when it ran into our minefields by mistake. No lives were lost because, being so close to shore, they were able to evacuate easily. Another sight that caught our boot sailor's eyes was the white crosses plotting a well-organized cemetery on a hillside, where many young men serving our nation had been buried underneath foreign soil.

We loaded up with provisions, including acorn butter from New Zealand and mutton from Australia and then departed for Efate, New Hebrides.

OUR ARRIVAL IN EFATE was exciting as we encountered a beautiful series of atolls and islands, some even mountainous. They were approximately 100 miles from Noumea, at the end of the Solomon Sea. The crew were assigned as guides on the port and starboard sides. Our captain had never experienced an entrance such as the Efate, Port Vila, approach. Our orders were to look out for rocky crags jutting out into the inland harbor. To this day, I have always wondered how this large array of huge warships ever cleared the rocky, craggy inlet, but they did. The fleet bombardment group had been shelling the Upper Solomons (Bougainville). The Caroline, Gilbert, Admiralty, and Marshall Islands had also been cleared in preparation for landing forces at a later date.

From his perch on the bridge, the captain skillfully sailed this steel monster through the rocks. With a little help from the deck and some praying, we came into a very deep island anchorage. The water was approximately 300 to 400 feet deep with an underwater atoll at a 160-foot depth. We were at the center of this so-called harbor. We dropped our starboard anchor at 29 fathoms (174 feet) and moved slowly to the center.

The chain dropped straight down until it finally hit the top of the underwater atoll. We dragged the anchor across and reversed down until we hung in mud or rock. With the ship finally fully at anchor, the anchor ball went up and the Navy Jack flew on the bow staff.

It was a Sunday morning in September 1943. As usual we had muster and a prayer session on the aft port side. Arthur Greenburg, our first class PHM (pharmacist mate), often conducted the daily prayer session. Being Jewish, he did not close the prayer "in Jesus' name."

This was a supposed secured fleet recuperating base for Navy and Marine personnel. The Malaysia and Tonga natives had moved their villages to the east side of the main island. The Seabees, the Navy's construction crewman, who usually landed with the Marines to follow up building airfields and digging graves, had bulldozed off a section of the main island for a recreation area, including a baseball field and volleyball courts. (Buster, the brother of my future wife, Yvonne, was a Seabee during the Pacific War.)

The bombardment group of the U.S. Pacific Third Fleet would arrive in five days. It consisted of six battleships, eight cruisers, twelve destroyers, and two carriers. In addition, it had two fleet oilers, two minelayers, and various support vessels.

As we were the first support vessel to arrive, our captain was honored as Superior Officer Present and Afloat, or SOPA. And there we were, in the middle of the Coral and Solomon Seas, not having seen any active battle yet, but it was clear that much had already happened around us. Our adventure through the Pacific war zone was just beginning and, in my case, wouldn't end until January 1946.

Chapter Twelve

ROBINSON CRUSOES

✳ ✳ ✳

WE HAD FIVE DAYS to enjoy this island paradise. The "Texas Four"—Carl, Ed, Shaw, and I—teamed up with Mick from New York, Cansler from Georgia, and Milton from Mississippi; the mess cook and an aft 20mm gunner were also in our group. We asked the captain for permission to tour West Island. It had a beautiful beach and heavy jungle terrain. The captain agreed, with the condition that we were not to roam out of sight of the ship. We all carried KA-BAR knives. Ed, our signalman and petty officer third class, carried a .45 automatic, a compass, and was designated the leader. We were told not to swim because the great white and gray sharks had been feasting on sailors, Marines, and soldiers for a year already but were still hungry. We were also instructed to be back on the west beach before sundown.

Our small Higgins ammunition lighter boat set us on the beach at 7:00 AM. We, the eight "Robinson Crusoes," hit the beach and shoved the Higgins off. Etheridge, the coxswain (the pilot of our little vessel), called out as he left, "Hey, guys. I heard through the saltwater grapevine that there are headhunters out here on the West Islands!" As adventurers, we laughed off that remark. The novel *Robinson Crusoe*, written in 1719 by Daniel Dafoe, was a popular read in my childhood and we all knew the story about an English castaway who lived 28 years on a remote South Pacific island, encountering natives, captives, and mutineers before being rescued.[4]

Ed, the only petty officer in the group, pulled out his compass and fixed a bearing on the ship. We headed south down the beach bordering the lagoon. We found no human tracks, only a javalina (a wild pig with sharp protruding tusks), and small deer. We gradually found our way into the bordering jungle, about 100 yards in. Ed sent Carl up a tree for a sighting. The ship was in sight and east of us. We moved up on a 10-degree slope. The jungle growth was mostly hardwood, bush bramble, and sparse vines. We saw small-animal paths, mostly with cloven hoofprints. This jungle animal evidence did not bother us, but

---

4   *Robinson Crusoe* is a fictional autobiography, where Dafoe presents an account of supposedly factual events to tell the story of the title character. It is sometimes regarded as the first novel in English.

the thought of Malaysian headhunters with poisoned blowgun darts was another problem.

Cansler scaled a large hardwood at the tip of the incline. He yelled down, "Ship in sight!" So, we moved a little further down the summit of the slope. We found signs that something fairly large had plowed a path through the treetops and appeared to be headed southwest down the opposite side of the summit.

Ed called a meeting, "What should we do at this point?"

We thought it over and decided that if a plane made this path and survivors existed, we could get aid.

Ed asked, "What if it's the enemy? How do we cope with it?"

It was obvious that a plane had crashed and found the jungle floor nearby. We agreed to investigate. In the excitement, caution and direction were forgotten.

Following the path of the plane crash was no problem. We began to find pieces of debris, rudder fabric, and a large tank that we identified as a seaplane float. It was painted a dull khaki color. This told us it was not a U.S. Navy floatplane, as they were painted a navy blue. U.S. floatplanes were normally carried on battleships and heavy cruisers as scout planes. This was quite possibly a Japanese or Australian scout plane.

The mystery was solved when we found a sheared-off section of a wing. The Japanese red rising sun was clearly visible. The discovery and the eagerness that followed quickly offset our schedule; ambitious and adventurous youth soon took hold, and we forgot our promises to the captain and the officer of the deck to stay within sight of our ship.

New danger might arise if the pilot were alive and armed. But following the rubble path, another wing sheared off on the port side, we finally found what was left of the fuselage, the main carcass, down the slope on the opposite side of where we landed. The fuselage was pencil thin, a very small pilot area, with a small pilot seat that would accommodate no more than a 130-pound person.

Since Carl and I had aircraft construction and repair training, the other sailors stood guard while we inspected the wreckage inside and out. The engine was a Mitsubishi or Suzuki 6-cylinder in-line liquid-cooled unit. All the instruments were fairly intact. The RPM, altimeter, fuel gauges, etc., indicated that no pilot was in the plane when it crashed. If there had been, then blood, hair, skin, teeth, or some evidence would have been strewn on the instrument panel. There was no fuel left in the wing tanks and they had not ruptured on impact.

Since Japanese pilots usually flew without parachutes, we surmised that he must have abandoned the craft over the water or jungle. If over water, the great white sharks in this part of the ocean made no distinction between race, color, or creed. If in the jungle, there was no indication of human habitation, at least on our journey to the crash site.

This floatplane was designed and built for one purpose: there was a bomb or torpedo pack under the fuselage—that indicated that this was a one-way suicide mission designed for a kamikaze pilot. A float under the rack would prevent a torpedo drop and the bomb would explode on impact.

We gathered around the wreck and decided there was nothing more we could do there. We decided to concentrate on finding our way back to the beach and eventually our ship. "Muscles" (Cansler) found a 40-foot tree, shinnied up about 25 feet, and reported seeing nothing but jungle. I asked Ed to give us a bearing on his magnetic compass. He fumbled around his knapsack and sheepishly reported, "I think I lost the compass, probably in the excitement of running down the hill to find the wreck."

He still had his Colt 45 automatic strapped to his belt, though. We all had our canteens and some wild bananas, and we felt we could survive regardless of being lost. The sun was setting and we thought north was back up the slope, so we headed in that direction.

Darkness came upon us quickly and the jungle began to close in all around us. The fear of the wild hogs, snakes, lizards, and possibly headhunters was beginning to affect our young, adventurous nerves. Our ages ranged from 18 to 21, and we all felt that we were tough and hardened. We were 10,000 miles from home, born in the 1920s, and had suffered through the Depression with hardworking parents. We were raised on oatmeal, cornbread, peanut butter, and pork. Out of the eight of us only four had finished high school, and that was the hard way. We earned money through paper routes and felt a deep sense of pride to be serving in the Navy of the greatest country in the world. None of our crew had seen any real action as of yet. Our baptism by enemy fire would be coming later at Bougainville, the Marianas, Iwo Jima, and, in my case, by the light of the beautiful Venus off of Okinawa.

Our immediate goal was to set up a campsite, build a good fire, organize a night watch, and hopefully be back to our ship before the Third Fleet arrived. Ed, the petty officer leader, assigned Milt, our steward, the first watch. Ed's cute remark was, "Milt will cover the area outside of the campfire glare. Since you're black, Milt, the headhunters can't see you and your Colt 45 in your belt, giving you first warning ability."

Milt retorted, "I may be black and have the black night around me, but, you know, the headhunters are also black and armed with blowguns and poisoned darts. Their weapon makes no noise, and one dead nigger won't be able to warn anybody!"

The conversation on assignments ended there. Carl had the first watch and the rest of us spread out, with Milt reassigned to the early morning watch. The jungle quieted down. The cockatoos, parrots, parakeets, and hundreds of other tropical birds made a lot of noise until complete darkness fell. After night descended, you could hear the rustle of brush and foliage. The movement of the leaves was mostly the wild hogs investigating the intruders in their jungle paradise.

If any of the natives ever decided to investigate our presence in their jungle, I am sure we would not have heard any noise. Long, sharp knives and silent blowguns would have made short work of their uninvited guests.

The assignment of watches was an exercise in futility. We weren't about to sleep out there. All hands spent the entire night gathering wood and feeding the campfire. At dawn one of our group, Jimbo, climbed a tree and reported a body of water about 10 miles northwest with a long peninsula jutting out on the west. There was no ship in sight. We were probably about four miles off course from our ship. We doused the fire and headed northwest. In about an hour, we came out on a beautiful, white-sand beach that faced a coral-loaded lagoon. There was no sign of life in any direction.

Ed pulled out his Colt 45 and fired off three rounds. It took only about 20 seconds to hear an answer, three shots from the other side of the peninsula. Twenty minutes later, our Higgins small ammo landing craft appeared. It came around the peninsula into the lagoon. Ed cautioned us to leave our shoes on and keep our sleeves and pants legs down. "It will help with the coral lacerations," he said. The lagoon was so full of the beautiful but jagged stuff that the rescue boat could only come in 50 yards from shore.

As Lex pulled us in, the ribbing began. He remarked that the captain was highly pissed off and radioed the Marine Air Force at Guadalcanal to start an air search for us. There was the possibility, after all, that the natives might have boiled us in their pots. His laugh told me he was just kidding. Back to the ship, up the companionway, wisecracks from our crew buddies resounded in our ears.

"Did you guys find the Long John Silver treasure chest?"

"Where is Robinson Crusoe?"

The officer of the deck met us at the deck landing and barked, "Follow me!"

We were eight very wet and hungry sailors, but we followed the OD to the forward #3 tank deck. The captain appeared and informed us that we would receive a Captain's Mast Court Martial for disobeying orders causing dereliction of duty. Fortunately, this type of court martial, before the mast, is a mild Navy slap on the wrist that later does not appear on one's record.

The captain couldn't help but laugh at our appearance, but he also informed us that in addition to our reprimand we would have to serve 24 extra duty hours on top of our regular duties. This was to begin after we fueled the Third Fleet, which was still on its way and would arrive within two days. All extra duty would be in the crow's nest watch, four hours each watch. Ed, our petty officer signalman, would serve his extra duty on the quartermaster's wheel.

Chapter Thirteen

VILLA

✳ ✳ ✳

T HE NEXT DAY, the OD passed Ed the word that a Marine group on the main island base had asked for volunteers from our ship to assist in erecting fun booths. Fun booths were structures such as dunking booths, ball-throwing at pins, beer booths, ice vats, washer pits, horseshoe pitching areas, softball fields, and basketball courts. Basically, they were any sport or activity that would keep the men busy while on recreation.

Since we were the only ship in the lagoon, we ended up with 25 volunteers. Our OD allowed 15 of us to go over and assist the Marine group with the recreation setup. Carl and I teamed up and made the volunteer group. The catch was that regular duties had to be in order first and each crewmember had a full 10- to 12-hour daily duty load.

We mustered on the cleared fleet recreation beach, and the 15 of us were split up into three groups of five. A Marine colonel assigned work details and the construction began. By noon we had four of the six fun booths erected, however rough. By 3:00 PM, there were two more booths, two beer booths, 30 rough four-legged tables, and four beer boxes. The battleships had icemakers in their large freezers and would furnish the ice.

All was ready for approximately 25,000 sailors and Marines to have recreation. Since no alcoholic beverages were allowed on U.S. Navy ships, the supply ships always had plenty of California, Acme, Schlitz, and Pabst Blue Ribbon beer.

A six-wheel truck rolled around and the driver asked for two volunteers to go with him to pick up the fleet mail at Villa, the French governor's small town that was approximately 22 miles from our beach. Sugar Sweeney and I jumped on the back of the truck and hollered out, "Take off!"

We traveled through the jungle on a bulldozed dirt road. After the fall of Guadalcanal, the New Hebrides islands were used as a "jump off" supply base for Marines and fleet units. Therefore, there were quite a few improvements made in these French island groups with the blessing of the free French governor.

While traveling the jungle road, we saw a few Melanesian natives loaded up to their heads with wild jungle foods. There was a bamboo pole across their shoulders with a bag on each side for balance, and they each had a machete hanging from their belt. They were moving along at a very fast pace.

We arrived at Villa at 3:30 PM and gazed upon a beautiful little French colonial town. It had a tropical lagoon, a small steamer in the harbor and the governor's quarter on a high hill overlooking the town. It was a scene from a storybook. The war with Japan seemed a long way off from this paradise.

There was a cobblestone main street with a few shops, a loading wharf, and an island prison that was no larger than 50 by 50 feet. Around this small prison were 10-foot concrete walls with broken wine bottles imbedded in the cement, jutting from the top of the wall.

We parked the truck at the dock and a motor launch came out from the ship with eight large bags of mail. We were at a loss as to why a French ship was handling U.S. Fleet mail. The driver explained that the French steamer sailed twice a week to Australia and brought the mail from the fleet APO (Army post office) in Australia.

We loaded the eight bags on our truck. The driver toured the town in about five minutes. He stopped by a small shop on the lagoon road. We all went inside and the driver hollered out a "Hello?"

A nice-looking lady appeared and greeted our driver, a Marine corporal, and pulled out a one-liter wine bottle and three glasses. The wine was a dark red French Cabernet and very dry. Sugar and I had not seen a white woman in three months, and we found this middle-aged, dark-haired French lady to be rather neat and attractive.

Next she brought out three pieces of cherry pie. This treat was well appreciated, and for a brief moment we felt like we were back home. She introduced herself to me and Sugar as Yvette Huevell, and she appeared to already be well acquainted with the corporal.

Yvette spoke fairly good English and asked, "What are you and Sugar doing in the New Hebrides?"

The corporal had cautioned us not to talk about the Third Fleet coming into Efate Lagoon so I told Yvette, "We stopped to drop off barrels of gasoline for the Marines."

Then, to change the subject, I asked her, "What about that prison? Why is there such a high-walled prison here in such a sparsely populated area?"

Yvette explained, "In the late 1930s, the island was a hideout for French citizens in trouble with the law, both criminally and politically. The governor organized a police force of French soldiers and a few natives to maintain law and order."

Evidently, the prison was built with a gallows inside the walls and even though the guillotine had been abolished, capital punishment was the remedy to discourse in this area. The governor was judge, jury, and executioner.

For payment, we left her two $2 bills. The Navy paid us in $2 bills each month. This nice French lady was very pleased with four U.S. dollars in cash. As we thanked her for the cherry pie, we jumped in the truck and looked back. Yvette was eyeing our large bags of mail. Ed had made it clear that she knew everything going on at the Marine base. She also knew that the base was closing and moving to Ulithi in the Central Pacific.

As we moved through the jungle back to our lagoon, the corporal explained "The Yvette Mystery." He told us that her husband, Paul, had been one of the criminal escapees from France who was hanged on the gallows at Villa in the late 1930s.

We arrived back at the Efate Lagoons at 5:30 PM and found the beach almost deserted. All booths were completed and rubble cleaned up. Our crew had been picked up and returned to the ship at 5:00 PM. This was another problem. I figured that being missing again would bring a more serious slap on the wrist. We noticed Everett, the coxswain, on the companionway ramp and waved our arms wildly. He sensed our plight and scrambled down to the motor launch. It was less than five minutes before we were on our way to the ship.

Our first question to Everett was, "Where are the officers?"

"Good question," he said. "They went over to the Officers Club earlier and are probably sleeping it off." I guessed that there would be no extra duty for me that day.

Chapter Fourteen

IRON BOTTOM BAY

✻ ✻ ✻

THE NEXT MORNING AT 6:00 AM, the boatswain blew his pipe and we filed into the mess hall. Being that it was a Saturday, we had our regular Navy beans with salt jowl, biscuits, Australian acorn butter, canned syrup, black coffee, and powdered milk.

We went to our duty station petty officers and received our individual fueling duties. On board I had recently completed the shipfitters rating and was now a third class petty officer. My duty was to check the forward pump room for leaks and pump fuel oil where needed. Descending to the bottom of the ship, I found that all valves were functioning. During my morning duties, we received by coded message that the Third Fleet was approaching the lagoon inlet.

When the ships began arriving, the eight heavy and light cruisers came first. Next were the battleships, led by the *Pennsylvania*, the flagship. The battleships *Maryland, Mississippi, New Mexico, Tennessee,* and the *California*, which had just left Pearl Harbor, were lined up in single file behind the *Pennsylvania*. Next came 12 destroyers of four different classes, two supply ships, and one minesweeper, followed by two fleet sea tankers.

This task force had been here before, and every ship found its anchor hole. We tied up the four destroyers and received orders to fuel two of the battleships. This scared the hell out of Captain Molinard. We had two battleships on either side of us, begging to be fueled. The captain was concerned because the design of these ships allowed for torpedo blisters to be welded to their port and starboard sides to minimize damage to the hull and engine room in case of a torpedo attack. We tried not to bump these blisters, which would have caused damage to our ship. We ended the fueling operation by 11:00 PM and our tanks were sucked dry.

While fueling, I was able to get the latest news from the sailors aboard the battleships. Most of them were survivors of the Coral Sea, Guadalcanal I, II, and III, and even Midway. Their tour consisted of heavy bombardment of Japanese strongholds in Truk, Rota, and New Guinea, New Britain. The next major campaign would be the Marianas and the Upper Solomon Islands.

The next morning, the battleships sent their bands and set-up crews to the beach. The supply ships set up the beer booths, and ship chaplains conducted early services on board. At 9:00 AM the launches started unloading crews on the beach. The plan was to allow approximately 12,000 men for the first shift.

The party continued the next day on the same schedule, with men taking shifts on ship and off. There was plenty of band and drum music. There was officer dunking (by volunteer, of course) and a bunch of dice games under almost every tree or bush. There were several fights, of course, which were promptly broken up by Marine and Navy shore details. One dice game brought on plenty of attention. A gunner's mate first class had a flour sack full of money—$5,000. The sailor stated that he would roll the dice when his sack of money was covered. He threw an empty flour sack on the ground. The hustle began. A Marine first sergeant started the collection of money, kept a record of money collected, and by whom. WWII service pay was not great; however, a 20% sea duty pay for serving in a war zone helped. Bills of U.S. currency began filling the sack. A second class yeoman performed the bookkeeping. In 45 minutes, the yeoman announced his count of $5,000. The gunner's mate rolled the dice four times. He won. He gathered the two sacks and a whale boat ferried him to the USS *Maryland*.

By Monday evening the brief vacation was over. Back on board, there were quite a few not-so-sober sailors, but it didn't matter. They were going back to sea. The destroyers were the first out through the slot, followed by the cruisers and battleships. The supply ships, tankers, and minesweeper followed the fleet. It was a grand sight to behold. We would meet some of the ships again on up the line at Bougainville, Saipan, Guam, and Iwo Jima.

We followed the fleet to Guadalcanal and broke with the two tankers to head to Tulagi to await merchant tankers. They were due from San Pedro, California, to load us up for further fueling duties. Merchant Marine tankers always brought the fuel to us, so it was not necessary for us to return to the States for oil. The next morning we arrived at Guadalcanal, steaming at full throttle across "Iron Bottom Bay."

This bay was named because of the air and naval battles fought in 1942, when Japan was winning the war. Fourteen ships were sunk in this bay. One Australian ship was counted with the many U.S. and Japanese ships buried there. Many Japanese and U.S. planes fought there as well. The story goes that the Japanese Navy's "Tokyo Express" came steaming through the Savo slot, their guns blazing, blowing our cruisers and destroyers out of the water. Our crippled fleet was heading for Espiritu Santo for repairs and refueling when a group of

class "I" Japanese submarines was waiting for them. As soon
as the crippled cruisers and destroyers were in range, the Japs
sent off their 21-foot and 24-foot torpedoes. One of those
torpedoes caught the cruiser *Juneau* straight center and the
explosion blew it in half, killing most of the crew.

The crewmen of the *San Francisco* later described the explosion: "The forward two turrets with their six-inch guns and
entire mount sailed 200 yards through the air and landed off the
stern of a destroyer." The *Juneau*, with over a thousand crewmen,
disappeared in 30 seconds. There were only 10 survivors, and
this explosion marked the death of the five Sullivan brothers, a
tragic loss for one family and an important incident that later
shaped the military assignments of family members in time of
war. The *Juneau* also went to her grave with $2 million in $2 bills
in her safe. The Navy's cash money for sailors was being paid in
$2 bills every month.

A torpedo severely damaged the heavy cruiser *New Orleans*,
too. Its bow was blown off and it moored close to the island,
camouflaging itself in jungle foliage until the submarine scare
was subdued. Then the crew of the *New Orleans* cut down coconut trees, lashed to the holes in the bow, enabling the ship to
cruise on into Espiritu Santo for repairs. She later participated
in every major battle from Tarawa, Enewetok, the Marianas,
Truk, and Rabaul.

During the three battles off Guadalcanal, the cruiser *Northampton* was sunk and the *Pensacola, Minneapolis,* and *New Orleans* were torpedoed. The destroyers *Guinn, Preston, Benham, Walke, Lamson, Lardner, Perkins, Fletcher, Maury,* and *Drayton* all opened fire on the "Tokyo Express." Several of those ships, heavily damaged, had to retire to Noumea for repairs. The battleships *South Dakota* and *Washington* opened fire and sank three major Japanese warships. The cruisers *Helena, Honolulu,* and *Portland* engaged 14 Jap destroyers and also suffered damage. The cruiser USS *Chicago* went down after an 18-inch shell from the Japanese battleship *Yamato* hit them. There were very few survivors.

Iron Bottom Sound was aptly named because of all the boats that sank there. As we sailed into this area in early 1944, we passed over the graveyard of ships. Very few white crosses appeared on the islands. Those who died on the water were buried there.

Chapter Fifteen

WASHING MACHINE CHARLIE

✳ ✳ ✳

AS I WAS HELMSMAN (quartermaster) on the wheel approaching Iron Bottom Sound, I pulled the wheel hard to starboard, as ordered. My pull was apparently too hard, as the boat almost started a complete circle. The captain roared, "Hard to starboard means 90 degrees from forward, not 120 degrees!" I quickly corrected the wheel compass reading to set our course right.

We slowed down to five knots upon entering Tulagi Lagoon. A free French corvette and frigates (a corvette was an armed patrol vessel, and a frigate was a smaller escort vessel) and two British destroyers were anchored nearby. We and the merchant tanker coming in from San Pedro, California, were warned of the underwater obstacles that awaited us.

We dropped anchor in 100 feet of water and posted full watch on the gangway and bow. Many Japanese soldiers and sailors who had escaped capture had melted into the jungle and were living in the native villages deep in the Solomon Mountains. Army and Marine detachments were based in outposts along the beaches but were ordered not to penetrate the interior for more than one mile. Other Navy craft were also stationed nearby. We noticed a PT boat squadron, a submarine diesel fueling dock out from the beach, and even a recreation area cleared for beer-drinking parties.

Our executive officer informed our crew of 79 men that Bob Hope and his group, who were now at Guadalcanal, would be brought over by PT boat to put on a show. We put up our movie screen and signaled the U.S. destroyers for a movie swap. We swapped two Robert Taylor films for two Gary Cooper ones.

No blackouts were planned while at Tulagi. The orders were not to fire on any Jap scout plane, a noisy craft that we dubbed "Washing Machine Charlie." The OD informed us at muster that the island command wanted the Japanese to know that we were now in charge of this end of the Solomons. We had paid dearly for this little orchard of coconut trees and jungle growth, and we intended to stay. The merchant tanker was due the next day and we would weigh anchor early Tuesday morning and head for deeper water. By dark, we had our Robert Taylor and Barbara Stanwyck movie going.

After about an hour, at approximately 8:00 PM, our general quarters alarm went off. The bridge watch hollered down, "Bogies! On the way from the north!" A bogy is an aircraft not identified as our own. We quickly shut the movie down and headed for our stations.

My station was a sight setter on the stern five-inch .38 caliber deck gun. Carl was hot shell man, Sugar was trainer, and Muscles was loader #1. Milt was loader #2 and Jim was the gunner's mate coordinator. Two stewards and a coxswain had the port 20mm aft and the deck crews had the other aft 20mm gun. It looked like we were finally going to see some action.

The aircraft was a "Washing Machine Charlie." We received orders from the bridge not to open fire until ordered from the bridge fire control man. Charlie clanked around overhead and none of us was firing. Evidently, the French corvette and frigate did not understand the orders. It was either that or the nightly wine allotment had been overextended, as the French opened fire with their 20mm guns, using tracers every seventh round.

They shot three holes in our crow's nest and hit our forward boom. Every ship in the area was signaling the Frenchies to cease-fire. Charlie never wavered and clanked on. He finally headed back north to one of the Japanese bases at Rabaul, Palau, Truk, or Rota. We secured "radar all clear" and continued our movie.

The next morning at 7:00 AM, we prepared to move further out into the bay for fueling room. As we started the anchor winch, the boatswain yelled out to the OD, "We're hung up on something!" Coming up slowly with our four-ton anchor was a Japanese plane, hung up on our anchor flange. I knew the Japanese plane IDs, as I had studied this at Algiers, and I identified what was left of it as a Mitsubishi Zero fighter plane. The fuselage was full of flak holes and the cockpit was empty. Sharks must have applied the coup de grace to the pilot.

The boatswain called for Carl to bring a fire axe. Carl, being our most physical specimen, very strong and agile and easily bench-pressing 250 pounds, was ordered to shinny down the anchor chain and ax-chop the wreckage away. He had to crawl over the fuselage and hang onto the chain while he chopped the skin of the plane. After he shinnied back up the chain, he told the boatswain to drop and raise the anchor. After two jerks the Zero returned to its grave in Iron Bottom Sound.

Our ship sailed about 400 yards into the bay, and dropped anchor to 60 fathoms (360 feet). We caught the bottom. The captain had a bad habit of dragging the anchor on the bottom until it sunk in the mud. We all passed remarks hoping that we didn't hang on a sunken ship hull.

We were anchored for about two hours. The tanker appeared coming to the west of Savo Island, the entrance to Iron Bottom Sound. In another hour he was beside us, coming up on our port side. Very slowly we threw out our sea bumpers fore and aft. After we tied ourselves snugly to the tanker, they passed over their hose lines and we transferred approximately 12,000 barrels of black fuel oil.

Later in the evening, when our four officers usually napped, we made deals with the merchant crews for a few bottles of Jack Daniels, Old Charter, and two quarts of blended scotch. Our bartering material was cigarettes and $2 bills. There were eight of us in on this trade. We hid the loot in the forward shipfitters shop, in between the anchor chain and the lockers. The merchant ship cut loose and headed for Pearl Harbor for supplies. After that, they were headed back to San Pedro, California, to reload.

At the next muster, 6:00 AM, we had our breakfast and noticed one crew member, Abdul Faro, an Arab draftee from Boca Chica, Florida, missing. He was a well-liked, jolly man who did not drink or smoke. He had had bouts of seasickness ever since we left New Orleans and was regularly excused from crow's nest duty for this reason.

The captain knew that he wouldn't attempt to swim ashore. There were too many fat and hungry great whites and grays in the lagoon. The only logical conclusion was that he had jumped ship and stowed away on the merchant vessel.

The problem was radioed by code to Pearl Harbor. They contacted the merchant ship and found Abdul in a lifeboat. They placed him on a destroyer to be confined in their brig. The destroyer was scheduled to arrive in Tulagi in a week. The edict from Pacific Command was that the deserter was to be returned to our ship and was our captain's responsibility. The captain was to confine the prisoner and schedule a court martial when the war permitted.

Our shipfitters group was assigned the duty of preparing the brig. There was a room on the second deck, above the engine room. It was only six feet by six feet and had a heavy steel door with a bronze Navy lock on the outside. For ventilation, we cut a 10-inch, round hole in the center of the door.

We were ready for our prisoner. The boatswain mate first class was assigned the duty of passing food and providing toilet necessities until the court martial was scheduled.

Chapter Sixteen

BOB HOPE

✵ ✵ ✵

THE BOB HOPE GROUP was due to perform at Tulagi the next day at approximately 1:00 PM, the hottest and most humid part of the day. We were in a part of the world where one could stand on so-called "dry land" and drown in his own sweat.

Carl, Sugar, and I planned a ringside seat on the beach for the show. We noticed a coconut tree about 30 yards from the makeshift stage. Our plan, if permission granted, was to take over supplies and rig a rope ladder to hang from for the show. This setup proved to be precarious, but we had nothing else to do.

With permission, we gathered our ropes and wooden cross-bars and had the coxswain take the first load over early. While moving along with 14 sailors aboard, I dangled my right arm over the side in the water to cool off. I heard a whisper, "Bring your arm in." Just as I did, something hit the side of the launch. The coxswain almost toppled into the water from the bump. A huge shark had caused the crash. After hitting us, he veered off, no arm in his jaws, and disappeared. This incident was a shock to us all, and there were no more arms dangling off the launch after that.

My personal feeling was that the whisper was from my guardian angel—my Grandfather Deal, who died when I was only four years old. Many times throughout my life I have heard a whisper say, "Don't do this" or "Stop. Go this way," or even "Stay away." That's why I have always felt safe, wherever I might have been. I believe that God assigned Grandfather Deal to me, and later on in my life my father, and for this blessing I will always be grateful.

After hitting the beach, we headed to work on our tree project while the launch returned for another load of sailors. Landing craft from other ships were already unloading sailors, Marines, and Coast Guardsmen. While we were erecting our temporary tree stand, a Marine lieutenant colonel came up and told us a story.

It seems that all of the coconut trees in the Solomon Islands belong to the Colgate-Palmolive-Peet Company and Lever Brothers, owned by the Australians. Under contract with the island protectorates, the trees were their property and should not be damaged in any way. He stated further that we could go ahead with the project because he doubted that the Australians could do much about it. He said that after we won the war, then the Colgate-Palmolive-Peet Company could have this miserable group of hellholes back to raise their coconuts. The colonel left with a brown bottle of Acme beer in his hand. War is not all hell and sometimes a little humor goes a long way in alleviating the fear of being consistently in harm's way.

We completed our tree rigging, and all three of us perched on the boards like crucified Christians. The PT boats moved into the lagoon with the troupe waving their hearts out to a bunch of young men a long way from home. The boats came alongside a makeshift log dock and headed for the stage. There was a canvas shield covering a section of the stage for some privacy.

Bob Hope and Jerry Colonna came out and stared at the coconut tree with the three of us hanging on for dear life. Bob's comment was, "If there are no monkeys on this island, then what the hell is that hanging from the coconut trees?"

The show was great, with Bob and Jerry making jokes for about 20 minutes. Jo Stafford sang three songs, and Frances Langford danced and sang. A chaplain closed the show with a prayer for all those who had died in the three sea battles at Iron Bottom Bay. The troupe sailed off for the Russell Islands next, with Bob yelling out, "Slap the Japs!"

We cleaned up our rigging and had our allotted four beers. We indulged in some games of craps, and by 6:00 PM our launch picked us up again. Returning to the ship, I kept my arms inside the launch. The next morning we headed for Bougainville, a German protectorate in the Upper Solomons. The Lower Solomons were French and British protectorates.

Two British destroyers came along for fuel. While topping off the Limey cans, we had an over-the-rail sailor-to-sailor session. They received grog (a mix of water and rum) daily after evening chow and had enough stored rum to fill four quarts in green corked bottles. They would let us have them for $10 U.S. per bottle. They would pick the time for the transfer of money and booze. When they called out, we shut our pumps off, and as we were drawing our lines a Limey appeared with a gunnysack. We exchanged our sack of money for their sack of rum.

Our captain dragged anchor to swing the ship around and headed seaward. We steered north by northwest for the Bougainville Straits and passed Savo, the Russells, and New Georgia. While we passed Savo, I was in the crow's nest, still having 16 hours to serve for missing muster. Each time the anchor winch began to rattle, one of our mates—Anchorball Jackson—headed to the rails. Seasickness was psychosomatic with Jackson, and sometimes he was sick before the ship even moved. It was common to see him at the rails.

I observed the east coast off of Guadalcanal and noticed six huge machines on the beach that looked very much like bulldozers; only the front blades were different. My binoculars gave me a good view of the beach. I called by phone from the nest and asked the OD if he could identify the machines. My curiosity was getting the best of me. Mr. Cross, the OD, was a congenial officer and remarked that he too was curious. He called me back about 20 minutes later. Our captain had heard through the Tulagi Officers Club that the machines were snowplows. They were destined for the Aleutians; however, the merchant ship made a mistake and dropped them off by barge with a few bulldozers. This was a spoils-of-war "boo boo," many more of which we would witness during our 27-month duty in the waters of the South and North Pacific.

Chapter Seventeen

ACTION

✠ ✠ ✠

WE MOVED ON past the Russell Islands and by twilight we were moving through the Vella Straits. (This was the spot where ***PT 109*** was sliced in half by a Japanese destroyer.) We discussed the "why's" of a wooden PT boat in Jap-infested waters. Our conclusion was that the PT boat playboys were having more fun playing yachtsmen than sinking ships.

After my watch, I gathered our booze crew and we retired to the shipfitters shop on the bow for a rum party. When we de-corked the first bottle, we tasted rum that was 90% water. The second, third, and fourth bottles were the same. We suckers decided then and there that those Limeys would pay! We filled a bunch of Acme brown beer bottles with a very unpopular drinking fluid and would charge those Brits $1 a bottle for them. We also spread the word about their trick and through our sailor pipeline of gossip the news was out, "*Don't* buy their rum!" Our plan was simple, and we knew we would see them again. They used our oil, our ammo, and our food and shared our recreation areas. The group of us was a very physical bunch. We had no doubt we would meet with those poor specimens of manhood again and that "our day would come."

At night we passed New Georgia and were close to Port Moresby, New Guinea. Army units were doing a fine job of mopping up these miserable jungles. Their casualties were heavy. The jungle took its toll, as did the Japanese soldiers sniping out of heavy jungle foliage. My brother-in-law, Earl Tillery, was with the 25th Division 35 Infantry second battery and he was somewhere in that jungle hell. Earl had married my sister, Charlene, in the early '40s. He was a home-delivery ice man, which meant he carried ice on his back door-to-door. While he was fighting the same war as I, Charlene continued to work back in Dallas at the Neiman Marcus lingerie department and as a model.

The next morning we sailed into the Bougainville lagoon. Several troopships were there already. There were supply ships, cruisers, destroyers, one aircraft carrier, one submarine, and, as this area was not yet secure, there was a lot of gunfire from the island. The island had been important to capture because the airfield allowed us a base of operations for medium bombers and long-range fighter-bombers, so we could keep hammering at the Japanese bases.

The Marshall and Gilbert Islands, including Enewetok, Tarawa, and Pelieu, were invaded and occupied at great cost in men, money, and material. Rumors over the saltwater pipeline were that this was mass preparation for the Marianas campaign.

We were directed by the Superior Officer Present and Afloat (SOPA) to anchor on the outskirts of the island. The reason was obvious. We were a tanker full of oil with barrels of diesel and high-octane topside. If a raid took place, then one spark and our burning hulk would light up the North Solomons like Fourth of July at Coney Island.

We began our fueling operations, and the general alarms went off on all ships and island forces. The alert message was that six Japanese medium bombers (bogies) were approaching from the northeast, probably coming from the New Ireland Japanese bases.

The great fear of all of the fighting men in the Pacific theatre was the fanatical suicide antics of the Japanese forces. The fear of dying was not in their Shinto religion. The fanatical will to serve their Emperor, right or wrong, was manifest—and being taken prisoner was a betrayal and a mortal sin. Throughout the Pacific theatre, our forces witnessed this fanatical will to serve until death.

The carrier could not launch planes, as it was at anchor and would have to be underway and heading into the wind, and with the Bougainville airstrip not yet ready for full operations, our guns, manned by hand, were our only defense.

The two-engine bombers appeared at 0800 as specks in the sky. They were about two miles out to the northeast. It appeared the targets were the island airstrips and tent bases. The bombers were spread out and not in formation, which made the single targets more difficult.

As sight setter on the five-inch .38, the elevation and fuse setting relayed from the bridge, the trainer was directed to lead the first visible bomber. When the brass was ejected, a hot shell man would catch the brass (he wore an asbestos suit) and place it in a metal box. At the same time, getting with another primed brass, the projectile man opened his steel box and set his fuse with a special tool. The brass man placed his shell into the rear cradle and the gunner's mate closed the breach hydraulically and fired the gun electrically.

We began to fire our five-inch and three-inch batteries, while the cruisers and destroyers had already opened up with their 40mm pom-poms. The cruisers couldn't fire because of their elevation. The sky to our east was filled with black puffs.

One bomber crashed on the base in flames. Another, on fire, headed for the carrier. All 20mm opened up a sheet of tracer steel and the bogy crashed about 100 yards southeast of the carrier. There is no doubt that a "Betty Bomber" kamikaze attempted to drop its load on the base and veered off to the east out of range. Another bomber crashed on the island, and three more left the area for their base to the northeast.

A total of three, identified as medium "Betty Bombers," had crashed. We expended three rounds each from our three-inch and five-inch batteries, but our 20mm's were quiet. All this action lasted about 25 minutes with no ship damage reported. There was quite a bit of damage to the airfield and base encampments. Two bulldozers were destroyed and five dump trucks. The Seabees had their work cut out for them. Most of the fleet units pulled anchor and put to sea, leaving one destroyer, our tanker, and one heavy cruiser. The APAs (combat troop carrier) and AKAs (combat cargo carrier) remained anchored.

✶ ✶ ✶

THE NEXT DAY, I asked our pharmacist first class to see if he could find a dentist on one of the troopships or the cruiser. I had an impacted wisdom tooth, badly in need of extracting. The closest heavy cruiser was the *New Orleans*, which had been at Pearl Harbor on that eventful date of December 7, 1941. On that day, her engines were under repair and they had power only from the yard generators. With inoperable guns, her crew, supplied with small arms by the gunner's mates, put up a good stand with 1903-30-06 Springfields and 45 Colt Autos. Eventually, a Jap fragmentation bomb exploding on deck caused serious injuries and damage.

After a trip to San Francisco for new search radar and new 20mm AA batteries, the *New Orleans* returned to the New Hebrides area with Task Force II of the Third Fleet. She was very active in the Coral Sea Battle.

Turns out, they did have an ensign dentist for me to see. Our launch dropped me off at their gangway landing. A seaman escorted me to the sickbay, second level forecastle. This very young ensign had a look at my wisdom tooth and remarked, "Yep, it's gotta go." He threw a towel over my chest and needled my gums on each side of the impacted tooth. No sooner was this done than the second general quarters alarm sounded, "Whoop, whoop, whoop." The ensign said he had to report to the bridge, "You stay in that chair until I return."

"Yessir," I replied.

The lone Japanese bogy was a high-flying scout plane. No shots were fired, as most of the damage on the first raid had been repaired, the holes covered on runways, the tents replaced, Seabees swarming with new bulldozers like nothing had happened. The fleet was out to sea, so the scout plane was allowed to return to Rabaul to make his report. "All ships in lagoon sunk," was probably the message sent to Tokyo.

The dentist returned and reached for his tongs. I said, "Please sir, would you re-deaden the tooth area for good measure?" This request he performed, never once washing his hands. The extraction, however, was still very painful. With a little sawing using a rotor carbide saw, the ensign finally forced the wisdom tooth out.

The next morning the fleet units returned for fueling. We fueled cruisers and destroyers; another tanker fueled the two aircraft carriers and the two battleships, the *Maryland* and the *Tennessee*. We had approximately 2,000 barrels left and were ordered to return to the Russells and unload on a stationary tanker barge deep in the jungle. Further orders were to sail to Pago Pago, Samoa, to take on a full load, plus deck barrels of diesel and high-octane gasoline.

At evening muster, this was explained to the crew by the captain. We were to receive further orders at Pago Pago. The Samoa assignment was good news. We'd get out of the islands of Melanesia to the islands of Polynesia, a well-known South Seas paradise.

In early 1944, the Pacific War was definitely in our favor. After the American victory at Midway, the Japanese lost their three main carriers and the fourth was heavily damaged. The main loss to the

Japanese was the cream of their carrier forces—their experienced pilots. Most all of them perished in the mid-Pacific seas.

As we steamed back to the Russell Islands, four destroyers from Squadron 23 screened us. Arriving at the Santa Isabel island group, we skirted the Russells and began the jungle lagoon journey, while the destroyers moved on to Espiritu Santo.

Steaming into Malaita Sound, we wondered how this 500-foot steel ship, 68 feet wide, drawing (at that time) 18 feet of water, would ever get through the lagoons showing up on our sonar at 35 to 45 feet deep. The skill of our captain in maneuvering us through this maze of narrow lagoons and jungle foliage was highly commendable.

We found the stationary hulk, an 1885 all-steel riveted sailing schooner. The masts had been cut off the forecastle about eight feet above the deck. All portholes were welded tight. This was a sight to behold. There were two 20mm AA guns. This hulk was about 22 feet wide and 130 feet long, with a crew of eight, all enlisted men. It had a chief petty officer in command, a gasoline-powered discharge pump, a small galley with a small fuel-powered stove, and a gasoline generator. A shallow draft supply ship from New Zealand kept them supplied with food, ammo, and cigarettes.

We tied up to two coconut trees on the fore and aft lines, dropped our hose over, and discharged our 2,000 barrels of diesel.

We left them Ken Maynard movies, some flour, cornmeal, and the other supplies they needed until their supply ship would arrive two weeks later.

The sailors aboard the schooner were loonies—sailors who had been too long in the jungle. They were due for rotation in two months. To date, they had spent 10 months in that isolated, mosquito-infested, hellhole of a jungle, their freshwater brought in on the supply ship. Since our evaporators were very proficient for a 78-man crew, we pumped over 1,000 gallons to fill their storage tanks.

There was a small Japanese Rising Sun decal painted on their forecastle. They told us that they had shot down a small Japanese scout plane with their 20mm's. It had crashed in the jungle about 500 feet north of them. Six of the crew explored the crash site and found the wreckage, but no pilot. They concluded that the natives had found him and carried him off, dead or alive. They did note that there was no blood in the cockpit. They had knocked his tail and rudder off with their 20mm's, causing the crash.

What was this old craft doing in the jungle? The crew's story made sense. During the late Solomon and Coral Sea campaigns in '42 and '43, the Navy desperately used every means possible to harass the Japanese effort to reoccupy the Solomons. This isolated fuel stop was used by the shallow draft destroyers (DDs), destroyer escorts (DEs), and PT boats to refuel and steal out of the jungle to harass the Japanese supply effort.

Our officers left some of their precious Old Fitzgerald bourbon (a Navy no-no) for the chief and his crew. We pulled out very slowly. We had no cargo fuel and rode high in the water. Our huge bronze screw slapped the water like a windmill in a typhoon. We took on ballast after leaving the jungle and steamed back to the Vella Strait. Our officers decided to move over to the Russell chain and give the crew shore recreation at the Marine rest base. This was announced at our evening muster and was greeted with hearty cheers.

Chapter Eighteen

SUBMARINE CONTACT

✶ ✶ ✶

ARRIVING AT THE RUSSELL ANCHORAGE, the crew was taken ashore for recreation. By late 1943, the island was well secured and the First, Second, Third, and Fourth Marine Divisions used the Santa Isabel/Russell Islands chain primarily for recreation stops.

The coconut plantations, planted like rows of corn by the soap companies in the '20s and '30s, were well organized. Any damage to the trees was to be charged to the U.S. government, and that was probably justified. However, the cost to those who made the supreme sacrifice, preserving the coconut plantations, was never considered!

Ashore, we made our way up the coconut grove road to the rest area. There was the usual shack for beer, some rough bunt tables, and ongoing crap games. Nearly all of the young boys who had joined the Navy had become beer drinkers, smokers, and gamblers, but there were very few atheists left. Everybody was a long way from apple pie and Mom's disciplined love. Every young sailor, Marine, and soldier thought about the big question: "Will I come out of this war alive?" Dying in the jungle or in the water, whichever way you leave this world really doesn't matter. It's what happens to your spirit/soul once you pass over that counts.

About 40 of our crew took our warm beers to a cool spot and drummed up a crap game to briefly forget the war. We continued to save our brown stubby bottles for our Limey allies on our next fuel meet. After an hour of losing $2 bills, Sugar, Carl, and I uncapped two more warm beers and joined a group of Marines in a shed covered with coconut leaves. Sugar, from Sugar Land, Texas, started asking questions of the young Marine group who were survivors—Third and Fourth Marine Divisions of Gilbert-Marshall campaigns, Tarawa, Kwajalein, and Enewetok. Our curiosity was met cheerfully.

They were in the decontamination squads. While they guzzled their warm beer, a corporal explained that their duties consisted of working with the Navy medics in identifying the remains of the dead and making preparations for burial. Once a plot was secured, Seabees would bulldoze an area. Graves were dug with a backhoe or by hand shovel. The corporal added that all bodies were placed in body bags. Another group was the ID squad and had registration responsibilities. We sailors had been briefed on procedures for burial at sea, and for sure, death at sea or on land leaves young minds fearful of what might happen tomorrow.

Sugar, Carl, and I finished our warm beer and mustered with our group. The petty officer in charge, Boatswain First Class Lawton already knew two would be missing. The two sailors had paired up and disappeared into the foliage. Soon they both re-appeared, casually walking to the landing, though not hand-in-hand. Lawton remarked that what went on while on recreation or leave was of no great concern to him. What took place on shipboard was his concern, and he would respond accordingly if any infractions occurred there.

We returned to the ship ready for the trip to Pago Pago, Samoa. We were hoping to be a part of the Marianas campaign. Our orders were to join the Third and Seventh Fleets at an unknown rendezvous in 32 days, with a full load of fuel.

The next morning, we dropped the anchor ball, weighed anchor, and headed through the Santa Cruz Straits, then the Tuvalu chain of islands. My quartermaster buddy, Causey, gave me a briefing as I was on the quartermaster wheel watch for two hours. We would steam up northwest through the Tuvalu chain, around Tokelau, west of this chain, and then into Tutuila, Pago Pago, the land of Polynesia. Our quest was to load on 11,000 to

12,000 barrels of crude fuel from the Samoa tank farm. Their oil supplies were brought in by Merchant Marine tankers from the Dutch West Indies (Aruba), through the canal.

The next day as we steamed west, coming up to the east side of Fakaoto, a small ship was detected by our radar approximately 10 miles to our north. The OD put his range finder scope on this ship and identified it as an "I" type Japanese submarine, cruising at approximately 15 knots.

Our speed was max at 12 knots.

The captain radioed by code for air coverage. We knew there would be no destroyer coverage because of the upcoming Marianas campaign. There was possibly destroyer escort craft at Samoa; however, we were 250 miles out from Tutuila.

Our ace in the hole was our five-inch .38 aft deck gun, with a range of six miles. If no carriers were in range, the nearest air patrols would be at Bougainville. Our gunnery officer calculated the "I" class sub could only cruise at 8 knots if submerged, 18 knots on the surface.

Our job on the five-inch .38 was to keep him submerged. He was closing in to a 7.2-mile range, out of his "Long Lance" torpedo range or his "kaiten" suicide human-guided mini-sub.

As sight setter on the starboard gun controls, I received the elevation and windage setting. The barrel responded. The trainer on the port side of the gun was given the "sight order," as we could now make out his conning tower and periscope mast.

We fired. The bridge reported a plume 100 yards off his bow. The hot brass was ejected, new brass and projectile set at surface detonation, a new elevation setting called in on my headphones. All set. The gunner's mate fired. The bridge reported that we were approximately 60 yards off his bow. We were closing in. A new elevation setting straddled the "I" boat. A total of five rounds forced him to dive and our goal was accomplished.

Even though we had no hit, the Japanese commander knew we would eventually score if he continued his surface run in our direction. No help arrived as we moved closer to British Samoa. Sixty miles east from American Samoa, they sent out a swordfish torpedo bomber and scoured the area to our rear, north by northwest. They made no contact. We figured the sub commander knew this part of the ocean very well and decided a fat, empty liberty ship was not worth a further risk.

Chapter Nineteen

TUTUILA

✳ ✳ ✳

A RRIVING AT TUTUILA, we maneuvered into a narrow lagoon. The town was on a semi-flat sand and coral plain, decorated with coconut trees, banana trees, bougainvillea, palm fronds, and beautifully landscaped roadways. The people were fair, olive-skinned, and beautiful, with perpetual smiles on their faces. These smiles were a wonderful sight compared to the more austere expression we had seen on the people of the islands of Melanesia.

We docked adjacent to a large-tank farm oil-storage facility. The local native Navy personnel wore unique uniforms: skirts called lava-lavas, which were tan with navy-blue stripes on the lower seams. One stripe appeared for apprentice seaman, two stripes for seaman second class, and three stripes for seaman first class. Petty officers had the Navy patch sewed onto their white

T-shirts; carpenters, metal smiths, and shipfitters had crossed hammers patches on their left arm.

Tutuila was a welcome respite from the Central Pacific war zone. The island seamen passed over their four-inch hoses; we hooked up fore and aft. Their pumps were high volume; therefore, we figured topping off our tanks by noon the next day. Half of our crew rated shore leave. You might say a quick island tour would be more like it. We didn't have much time, as we were scheduled to leave for the Marianas at 8:00 PM with a British corvette from British Samoa for escorting to 00.00 latitude, 88.00 longitude (equator). Our officers planned our crossing the equator as a major production, elevating the majority of the crew from pollywogs to salty "shellbacks"—all sailors become shellbacks by crossing the equator by sea.

Though our Samoan island tour was fun and educational, I did not get to achieve one of my personal goals of visiting the gravesite of Robert Louis Stevenson, the Scottish novelist, poet, and travel writer, and author of *Treasure Island*.[5] His grave is located about 10 miles inland on the island of Upolu and marked by a stone tablet with the famous requiem he always intended for his epitaph:

---

5   *Treasure Island,* by Robert Louis Stevenson, was first published as a book in 1883. It is one of the most frequently dramatized of all novels.

Under the wide and starry sky,
Dig the grave and let me lie.
Glad did I live and gladly die,
And I laid me down with a will.

This be the verse you grave for me:
Here he lies where he longed to be;
Home is the sailor, home from sea,
And the hunter home from the hill.

—ROBERT LOUIS STEVENSON (1850-1894)

I would have liked to pause there a while, but our schedule was just too tight once we received orders to head back to the Marianas.

Tutuila was full of beautiful people with beautiful bodies. We did have time to visit a few pubs, drink a few glasses of wine and some Australian beer, and take a few photos of island beauties before returning back to the ship and out to sea.

Our group reconsidered the revenge plan against our Limey friends. After all, they were our allies, plus they could be saving our lives by their escort effort. Submarine commanders have great fear of depth charges. We felt safer with that little Limey vessel 300 yards off our port side.

Our few shellbacks made some preparations for initiating the 65 pollywogs:

1. Our heads would be shaved by the shop's barber.

2. We were to crawl through a 12-foot canvas bag, 20
   inches in diameter with a saltwater hose spewing at
   the exit end. If you came out the hose end, you were
   very lucky. A few of the pollywogs almost drowned
   in the canvas bag. This ordeal lasted two hours,
   leaving a funny-looking crew with bald heads and
   red eyes.

If a Japanese sub commander had had his periscope on our
ship, he'd probably have felt sorry for us. We looked more like a
tramp merchant ship not worthy of his expensive torpedo.

We steamed on into the Phoenix Island chain, through the
Gilbert chain, passing Tarawa, then Little Makin. Approaching
the Marshalls, we ran into a small typhoon and swells up to 25
feet high. We maintained our watch schedule with our full load,
drawing 28 feet of water.

The boatswain secured the crow's nest and ordered Joe Cel-
line, the watch, to descend to the deck. Joe, on coming down the
straight one-inch rung steel ladder, lost his grip and fell about
20 feet, landing on his shoulder. Our doctor, Art Greenberg,
ordered Joe to be taken to the sickbay, where he eased Joe's pain
with morphine. Since we had no x-ray facility, Art's diagnosis
was possible heavy fractures to the back and shoulder blades. As
we were steaming into the Marshall Island chain, our captain
hoped to contact a hospital ship, as Kwajalein, Enewetok, and
Bikini had earlier been secured by Marines.

While on our South Seas journey, the Third, Fifth, and Seventh Fleet Task Forces and Third and Fourth Marine Divisions had invaded Guam, Tinian, and Saipan. There was a heavy loss in ships, sailors, and Marine casualties. The combined assault on the Marianas in June 1944 was tabbed as the Great Marianas Turkey Shoot. The Japanese forces sailed in from their Borneo bases through San Bernardino and, detected by U.S. submarine forces, were reported to the Fifth and Seventh Fleets. The Third Fleet moved in from Guam, intercepting Admiral Ozawa's strike force. The turkey shoot began.

We were five days off from this area, receiving coded messages as to what was going on. Our orders were to avoid this area until Saipan was secured. During the sea battles, the Marines were hitting the beach at Guam, Tinian, and Saipan.

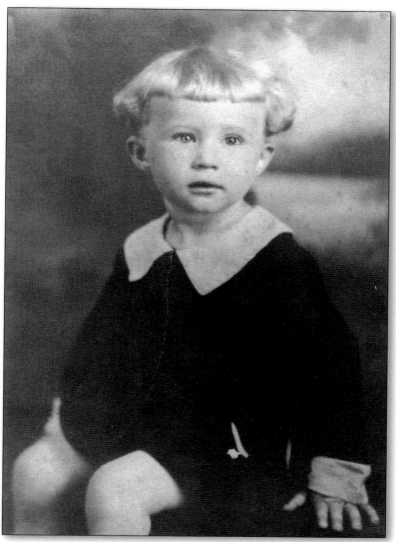

Harry William Deal (age 4), *1925*

Charlene (age 11) and Harry (age 9), *1930s*

Emma Skidmore Merrill,
Harry's great-aunt, *circa 1900*

May Skidmore Deal *(1895–1987),*
Harry's mother (age **39**), *1934*

Charles William Deal III *(1885–1952),*
Harry's father (age **45**), *1930*

Harry (age 21), upon enlistment
in the Navy, *1942*

Arthur "Jabo" Tillery and Harry, upon completion of boot camp, *1942*

Navy Day Parade, Dallas, Texas, December *1942*

Navy Day Parade, Dallas, Texas, December *1942*

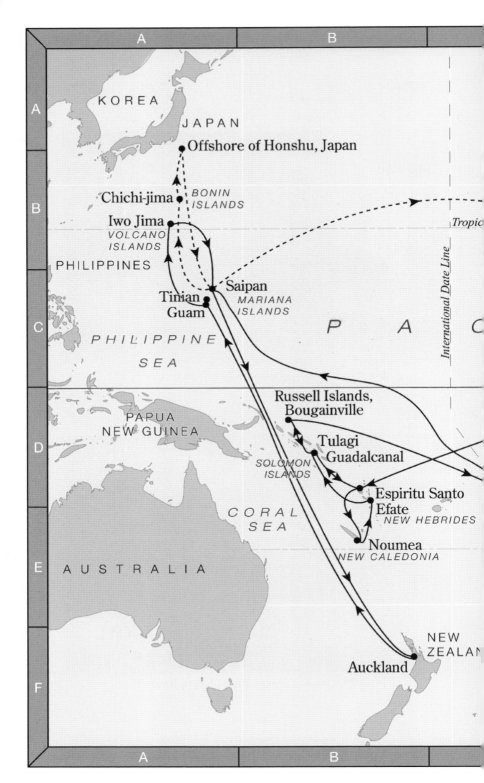

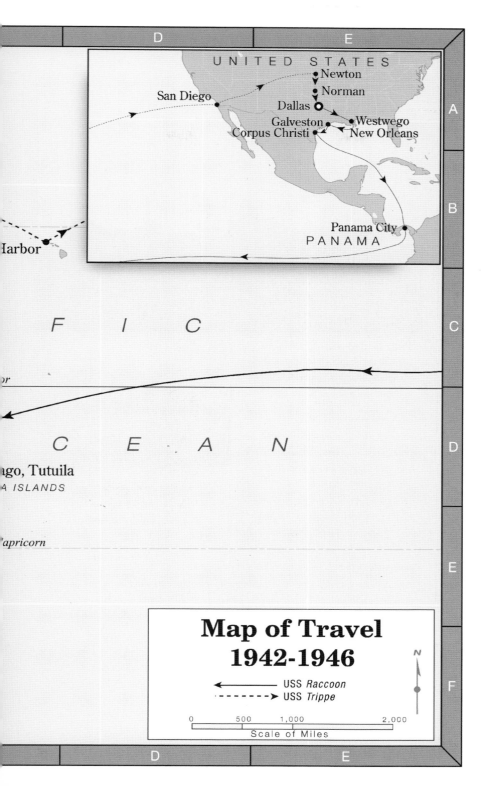

UNITED STATES

Newton
Norman
San Diego
Dallas
Galveston
Westwego
Corpus Christi
New Orleans

Panama City
PANAMA

Harbor

F I C

or

C E A N

ago, Tutuila
A ISLANDS

apricorn

Map of Travel
1942-1946

N

⟵ USS *Raccoon*
⤙------▶ USS *Trippe*

0   500   1,000   2,000
Scale of Miles

Fully loaded with 12,000 barrels
of oil and high-octane gasoline,
USS *Raccoon*, Tinian, 1944

- *USS* **Raccoon** *(IX-127)*
- *Built in Delta shipyards, New
  Orleans, Louisiana, 1942-1943,
  and was assigned as a Merchant
  Marine cargo vessel.*
- *1943 converted to oil-gasoline, diesel.
  Five tanks with pump rooms fore
  and aft. Crew of 74 enlisted men and
  5 officers.*

USS *Porcupine*, **sistership of**
USS *Raccoon*, **sunk in 1944
at Leyte Gulf, Philippines**

- *Assigned to the U.S. Pacific Third Fleet.*
- *Armament: One five-inch .38 caliber deck gun aft, one three-inch .50 caliber
  forward deck gun, eight 20mm (four port, four starboard) as anti-aircraft
  rapid-fire guns, two .50 caliber machine guns on the bridge. Small arms: twelve
  .30-60 rifles, twelve 1911 .45 caliber autos. Ten flare guns.*
- *Four whaleboats and eight life rafts.*
- *Campaigns from Guadalcanal to Iwo Jima and Honshu.*
- *Traveled 200,000 nautical miles in South, Central, and North Pacific.*

Crossing the equator on the
USS *Raccoon*, 1943

Muster on the way to Efate, USS *Raccoon*, 1943

Muster on the way to Efate, USS *Raccoon, 1943*

Earl Tillery, Harry's brother-in-law,
New Guinea, *1944*

Indigenous Samoan men sitting outside a *fale* (traditional open house without walls), Pago Pago, Solomon Islands, *1944*

Samoan dancer, *1944*

Deck crew, USS *Raccoon*, Russell Islands, January *1944*

Ed Tooley, "Anchorball" Johnson, and Harry on board the
USS *Raccoon*, Iwo Jima, *1945*

Shipfitters gang, USS *Raccoon*, *1944*

Mount Suribachi, Iwo Jima, *1945*

Landing at Iwo Jima, *1945*

Squadron 20, moving toward Iwo Jima, *1945*

USS *Trippe* **en route to Japan,** *1944*

- USS **Trippe** *(DD-403)*
- *Built in Boston Navy Yard, 1938, Gridley Class*
- *Number changed from 411 to 403 in 1942 and re-outfitted in 1943.*
- *Served in the Atlantic Fifth Fleet, 1940–1944.*
- *Transited the Panama Canal 1944 and joined the Third Fleet.*
- *Served in the Pacific Third Fleet, 1944–1946, Saipan, Iwo Jima, Okinawa, Honshu.*
- *Battle record: Sunk four Nazi submarines; bombarded Anzio, Normandy, Sicily, Corsica, Africa, Iwo Jima, and Honshu.*

USS *Enterprise* **being torpedoed, Battle of Midway,** *1942*

UNITED STATES NAVY

My dear Mrs. Deal,

I've just returned to the states from duty aboard the U.S.S. Raccoon, where I enjoyed the friendship and confidence of your son Harry— I promised him that I'd write to you when I got here, hence this letter— Harry was in the best of health when I left the ship— I know 'cause I was the "Doc"— We enjoyed liberties together at Tulagi— Florida Island— Espiritu Santo and Efate and Panama— He's one chap you may well be proud of— It hurt me to leave that ship because I had so many friends like Harry aboard—

Do send him my regards when you write—

Arthur A. Greenberg PhM1c.

**Letter from Pharmacist Mate 1st Class Arthur Greenberg
to Harry's mother, May Deal, July 1944**

SF 3/C HARRY W. DEAL
U.S. PACIFIC 3rd FLEET
U.S.S. RACCOON - 1 X 127
U.S.S. TRIPPE DD 403
1942 - 1946

Harry's WWII medals and memorabilia

THE SECRETARY OF THE NAVY
WASHINGTON

February 5, 1946

My dear Mr. Deal:

I have addressed this letter to reach you after all the formalities of your separation from active service are completed. I have done so because, without formality but as clearly as I know how to say it, I want the Navy's pride in you, which it is my privilege to express, to reach into your civil life and to remain with you always.

You have served in the greatest Navy in the world.

It crushed two enemy fleets at once, receiving their surrenders only four months apart.

It brought our land-based airpower within bombing range of the enemy, and set our ground armies on the beachheads of final victory.

It performed the multitude of tasks necessary to support these military operations.

No other Navy at any time has done so much. For your part in these achievements you deserve to be proud as long as you live. The Nation which you served at a time of crisis will remember you with gratitude.

The best wishes of the Navy go with you into civilian life. Good luck!

Sincerely yours,

James Forrestal

James Forrestal

Mr. Harry William Deal
3736 Dixon St.
Dallas, Texas

Letter of "Gratitude of the Nation" to Harry
from the Secretary of the Navy, *1946*

O.L. Rivers, Yvonne's brother,
1939

Earl Tillery, Harry's
brother-in-law, *1942*

Glendon Rivers, Yvonne's brother,
1944

Bobby Ray Rivers, Yvonne's
brother, Korean War, *1953*

Yvonne Frances Rivers, *1943*

Yvonne and Harry on honeymoon, *1947*

After the war, with family: Yvonne, Harry, Betty Jo Deal, Charlene, and Charles William Deal (Harry's father), *1947*

Family portrait: Harry and Yvonne with children Beverly, Stephen, and Suzanne, *1956*

Beverly, Stephen, Suzanne, and Yvonne at the San Jose Mission, San Antonio, Texas, in August 1956, where Harry and his sister Charlene used to play as children

Beverly, Stephen, Suzanne, and Harry at the
San Jose Mission, 1956

**Harry in front of the Pearl Harbor Memorial,
Washington, D.C.,** *May 2004*

**Harry with daughter Suzanne Deal Booth and grandson Chandler Booth
(age 7), WWII Monument Dedication, Washington, D.C.,** *May 2004*

Chapter Twenty

KEEP MOVING

✴ ✴ ✴

W E ABRUPTLY CHANGED COURSE to steam into the Caroline Islands for a new base, called Ulithi. The Espiritu Santo repair base was being moved there and a Navy hospital ship was at anchor. This diversion took us out of the typhoons and into calmer waters.

We picked up a destroyer escort (DE682) and proceeded on into the Carolines. The DE left us at Namonuito. We arrived at Ulithi, anchored near the hospital ship, launched our motor launch, and transported Joe to a first-class medical facility. The two Navy nurses waiting at the gangway couldn't help but laugh. They tried very hard to suppress their amused grins. Our doctor had made a one- by three-inch board cross, taping the vertical board to Joe's neck and back above the hips. The horizontal board was taped to each shoulder blade and under the upper arms. Joe looked like he was hanging on a cross. We nicknamed him "Jesus Joe." He had no objection and good-naturedly went along, only too happy to be getting help and later shore leave as the hospital ship was scheduled to leave for San Diego the next day with wounded Marines. We proceeded on to another anchorage to await further orders.

A squadron of destroyers arrived from Pearl Harbor, re-fueled, and dropped off our missing man, Abdul Faro. Abdul looked very pale after being in brigs for six months. The boat-swain took Abdul down to the brig, his new home for a while. The responsibility of the Summary Court Martial for desertion was on the backs of our captain and his officers.

In the meantime, the war continued. The reports, via the saltwater pipeline (Navy rumors and talk), were positive. Some light on Pacific Naval war history accordingly points out our losses in 1942 and 1943 as very significant. With the loss of the *Hornet* and *Wasp*, our fighting Navy was down to one crippled carrier, the *Saratoga*.

The Japanese submarine force with their "Long Lance" tor-pedo was very formidable to deal with. However, reports from destroyer sailors were complaints that U.S. Navy torpedoes did not always explode on contact. Only five out of nine exploded. One destroyer crew reported that in the sinking of the USS *Hornet*, their squadron fired nine torpedoes before finishing off the crippled and burning carrier. Another squadron reported over the rails that when the *Princeton* was hit by a Japanese 500-pound bomb, the cruiser *Birmingham* was almost devastated by the exploding carrier ordinance while trying to rescue survivors. Their loss in manpower was heavy. The destroyer USS *Shaw* was almost wiped out when a forklift fell off the *Princeton* onto the *Shaw's* bridge, after survivors were rescued. Orders were given to sink the *Princeton*. One destroyer launched torpedoes that, after 500 yards heading for the carrier, reversed course and headed for the destroyers. Luckily, they outran the faulty torpedoes with a speed of 37 knots. Bad things do happen in war. Men die from friendly fire as well as enemy fire.

Our refueling complete, we had about 6,000 barrels left in our tanks. We were ordered to Guam, supposedly secure at this time. While steaming north by northwest to Guam, we would be almost in the heart of Micronesia. After shore recreation at Mogmog, our impression of the local natives was that their skin color was lighter than the Melanesians, and darker than the Polynesians. This was perhaps due to the mixing of races over the previous generations as many Christian missions had been established in these islands.

Regarding religion on board, the crew was mostly Christian with a few Orthodox Jewish boys and one Muslim (in the brig). It is amazing how men find their faith under fire, and after our participation at Iwo Jima we all seemed to be devout believers in a god, be it God, Jesus, or Allah. We were all praying non-stop it seemed, and the believer level scaled out to about 100%!

Abdul was content in his iron room. He did not smoke or drink alcohol, and his appetite was good. Once in a while we would slip him some extras—mostly sweets, chocolate bars, donuts, or coffee at all hours. We told him we were about three to four days out of Guam, his court martial rendezvous. He had already resigned his fate to a jail or prison sentence for wartime desertion, with the remark now and then, "Allah will take care of me."

Our food supply was fairly good—turkey, chicken, plenty of beans, very few eggs (dehydrated mostly), dehydrated potatoes, Spam, and cornmeal and flour full of weevils. In a humid, tropical climate, ground meal breeds weevils. During meals, we would count the weevils per slice. The sailor with the most brown specks would win a prize—usually a Hershey bar or donut. Our oatmeal was pretty clean, with very few specks; powdered milk with speckled sugar and speckled toast was the standard breakfast.

We had canned fruit juice from California and Florida and plenty of coffee. Meats were mostly mutton from Australia and New Zealand, canned meats, salmon, sardines, tuna, and occasionally K-rations.

✻ ✻ ✻

Chapter Twenty-One

REALITIES OF WAR

✳ ✳ ✳

WHILE AT ULITHI, I interviewed a submariner and when I described the Japanese small float plane we found in the jungle at Efate, he solved the mystery of why that Jap plane might have crashed there. The Japanese had designed six large, A-I-400 class submarines as underwater aircraft carriers. This light float plane was folded into the hull, wings detached, and assembled while on the surface; it would carry only one medium-sized torpedo. The subs would maneuver to within 200 miles of the Panama Canal; then the plane and pilot would make a one-way trip to the canal locks. A suicide dive would cripple five to six locks and bottle up the canal for two years. The I-400 submarines were mustering at Truk and Rabaul naval bases being readied for this operation.

Admiral Spruance had other plans for these Japanese bases and sent carrier-based torpedo bombers, Hellcats, and Douglas dive-bombers in droves, devastating these two Japanese Central Pacific strongholds.

The Japanese subs that were put to sea under cover of darkness were detected by a squadron of destroyers and destroyer escorts. These escorts were equipped with the new "hedgehog" depth charges, which when launched would hold together until five seconds before hitting the water and at which time they would split up into a fan of charges covering a 50-foot diameter section of ocean about 30 to 40 feet deep. This effort destroyed the Panama Canal project for the Japanese Navy. My sub sailor informant surmised that the crashed float plane was probably on a training flight earlier in the war when he went down in that area of the South Pacific.

Reports from other fleet sailors brought us up-to-date on the Marianas Turkey Shoot in the waters of Guam, Tinian, and Saipan. This series of sea battles left the Japanese Navy almost devoid of aircraft carriers. They lost two carriers, two cruisers, two destroyers, and one tanker. This battle was fought mostly by the two fleets that never visually observed each other. Mostly aircraft, our carrier fleet had grown from two old carriers in 1942 to over 80 in 1944. The Japanese lost the cream of their carrier pilots with 395 planes shot down. We'd lost 130 planes and 76 pilots. The Japanese abandoned the Midway landing and retreated to Formosa.

The Marianas campaign almost voided the Japanese Navy as a formidable fighting force. But this battle was another air war. The ownership of power in the Pacific was now in our favor. Yet, the occupying of the islands by the assault Marine forces was at a heavy price: Guam; Tinian, with fewer casualties; Saipan had heavy losses. This island had been in the Japanese prefecture for 300 years. A home island defended to the death.

✳ ✳ ✳

FROM JANUARY TO JUNE 1944, the submariners reported their fleets sank 492 large cargo ships and destroyed one-third of the Japanese combat ships in Central, North, and home island Pacific. The ocean was ours. We owned the South, Central, and a large chunk of the North Pacific.

My diary journal was filling up fast. I kept the book under my mattress because everything we wrote was censored. My mother wrote me a letter letting me know that one whole line in a letter I had written her had been blacked out. I remember jotting down the number of barrels of oil we had pumped into the battleship *Tennessee*, as if the Japanese Navy really cared. They were too busy running and protecting what fleet they had left.

We arrived in Guam in late June. In a few short weeks the Seabees had erected log docks for supply landings. The Seabees were the can-do battalions. While under fire, they accomplished wonders. Our fleet, our Marines, or Army, and Coast Guard were all can-do personnel. Nothing could stop us. I would not have missed this journey across the seas for anything. According to rail talk, a Japanese admiral remarked after Pearl Harbor: "All we have done is to awaken a sleeping giant." Their defeat at Midway proved that to be true.

It was a wonderful experience to have played a big part in helping to destroy the huge Japanese war machine. However, the war was not over, as we still had a long way to go to conquer this country. Many more men would die on the water and the beaches. The Japanese did not have the word "surrender" in their language, and at every landing the price we paid in young lives began to haunt the High Command.

While at Guam, Abdul was delivered to the CINPAC (U.S. Commander-in-Chief in Pacific) for trial (desertion in wartime). Our captain would deliver the charges and a naval court (a five-man court of inquiry, a defense and prosecution officer, and a five-man jury) would decide the penalty. The trial lasted two days, and a very light sentence was handed down based on Abdul's reason for desertion. His plea was, "I was drafted and had no desire to fight in a war against a people that did me no harm personally." He was to be shipped to the Federal prison at Pearl Harbor, to be confined until the war ended, and six months after the war ended to be dishonorably discharged and sent home to Boca-Chica, Florida.

While we were moored to the dock at Guam, I sought permission to visit the Marine garrison on the east end of the island. We had several friends from South Dallas who had joined the Marine assault battalions—the Third, Fourth, and Fifth Divisions—who had made landings at Tarawa, Kwajalein, Enewetok, as well as participated as reserves in the Tinian, Guam, and Saipan landings. Marines were scattered around on mopping-up operations on all three islands in the Marianas.

Finding the divisional headquarters was no problem. Carl was with me and we caught a Jeep ride to the tent headquarters on Guam. The base commander was at Saipan, because of stubborn Japanese guerilla resistance. Tenth Army units and Marine reserves were still facing small arms fire, as all the enemy artillery was destroyed. The Marine lieutenant in charge explained that, as of July 1944, the enemy loss at Saipan was at 4,300 dead and a few prisoners. Our losses were at 1,500 killed in action, with 12,000 wounded. The enemy was very stubborn, fanatical, fighting to the death, charging Army and Marine machine gun nests screaming, "Banzai!"—the Gyokusai, "death with honor" and "seven lives for the emperor" code, at first practiced on Attu, in the Aleutians, and now at Saipan and Tinian.

A Marine sergeant in the headquarters told of his experience at Tinian. He had his .30-06 caliber air-cooled gun set up at the edge of the Japanese airfield. Their goal was to capture, not kill, the enemy. His assistant's beltfeeder and his gun were on the ready. All of a sudden a horde of Japanese soldiers appeared—led by two Samurai sword-wielding officers screaming 'Banzai!'—and charged their line.

"We opened up—my gun, an LVD, another 30.06 machine gun 50 yards from mine, and 150 Army and Marine infantry riflemen along our line. They kept coming, running over their dead, one battalion after another, screaming, 'BANZAI!' After 30 minutes of this fanatical waste of life, the battle was over. Our casualties were five dead infantrymen and 30 wounded. The enemy toll, out there in piles, was 300 dead, no prisoners."

The sergeant said, "The enemy could have spread out his men in the cane and bamboo breaks, and with sniper action could have wiped us out. The Japs outnumbered us four to one."

The lieutenant explained to Carl and me that the burials had not been completed on Saipan, Guam, or Tinian, and that the names of the dead could not be divulged until all were fully and accurately identified and the next of kin notified properly.

He also explained that no bodies were to be left on the islands. As soon as the war was over (and we all knew who was going to win this war), all bodies would be eventually moved to the National Cemetery in Hawaii. The Pacific Army and Navy Chiefs of Staff had decreed that no American bodies would be left in the battlefield cemeteries, from the Solomons, New Guinea, the Gilberts, the Carolines, the Marshalls, the Marianas, and other forthcoming battle casualties in this Pacific War.

Carl and I returned to the ship, as we were scheduled to steam for Saipan the next day. We pumped 8,000 barrels of oil to eight destroyers and four cruisers over a three-day period. One of the cruisers was the USS *Indianapolis*, sunk by "I" boat torpedoes two days after leaving Saipan.

Chapter Twenty-Two

SAIPAN

✳ ✳ ✳

T HE SALTWATER PIPELINE fed us the approximate Navy losses in the Marianas Turkey Shoot. The Japanese task force came in from Leyte, Truk, and Rabaul in force. Our carriers, aware of their approach, stopped our landings on their home islands, namely Saipan and Tinian. Guam was a U.S. possession and occupied by the Japanese after attacking Pearl Harbor. To meet this force, we launched 300 to 400 aircraft loaded with 500- and 1,000-pound bombs, torpedoes, and .50 caliber armor-piercing ammo.

After three days of mostly air action, the enemy lost two carriers, two destroyers, and two tankers, with 11 of their major warships damaged. Their greatest loss was the 395 aircraft and a like number of their best pilots, plus 31 float planes, 50 planes on Guam, and 30 warplanes on Saipan. As noted, U.S. losses were 130 planes, 76 pilots, two battleships, and one aircraft carrier heavily damaged.

The sunken Japanese warships that went down in the Marianas waters, 12 miles deep, probably never reached the bottom intact. The pressure at 8,000 pounds per square inch would crush them like stepping on a cocktail glass. The Japanese fleet abandoned the battle and limped back to their bases at Formosa. The Seabee battalions landed and began to prepare Guam, Tinian, and Saipan airfields to land heavy bombers—the B-24 Liberators, superfortresses, B-29s—and B-25 and A-20A medium bombers.

Later, the huge B-29 superbombers to be based at Tinian and Guam would literally destroy the home island of Japan proper. We steamed into the Saipan anchorage and awaited a merchant tanker from Long Beach, California, to take on a full load of cargo oil.

Saipan was a Japanese home island and was defended to the bitter end. It contained very few prisoners, mostly Korean slave laborers. The Japanese Army used the Koreans as cannon fodder and would arm the Koreans with old rifles and force them out in the open to draw fire from the Marines. Many would throw up their hands to surrender.

There was quite a bit of small-arms fire, no artillery, as the Marine and Tenth Army units had destroyed all the gun emplacements. The stench of death covered this island. Blood-sucking flies, as big as quarters, landed on our decks and when you stepped on one it popped like a balloon.

There were two carriers in the anchorage along with two battleships—the *Indiana* and the *Tennessee*—four cruisers, and eight destroyers. The carriers were performing their usual maintenance program; any planes that required major repairs were pushed over the side. The water where they were anchored was about 250 feet deep.

The Marianas Turkey Shoot was an aerial war, and our warships were doing a very good job of clearing the skies with their AA units. They could paint the sky black with their 40mm and 20mm AA units. While we were awaiting our loading tanker from San Pedro, our sister ship, the USS *Porcupine,* arrived. The *Porcupine,* or IX-126, had left New Orleans two weeks before we sailed. We were the IX-127. Their usual cargo was 100-octane aviation gasoline for the carriers and two tanks of diesel fuel for landing craft. They too were empty and awaiting a merchant tanker from Long Beach for loading their high-octane.

The *Porcupine* anchored about 400 yards north of us, close to the carriers. We were happy they were not closer to us because, once fully loaded, one spark and they would light up the whole island and harbor.

✻ ✻ ✻

Chapter Twenty-Three

GARAPAN

✳ ✳ ✳

To ENHANCE MY DIARY, I asked permission to go ashore to tour the secured areas and was assured the town of Garapan was safe. The Japanese commander of the Garapan defense forces had spread propaganda that U.S. Marines and Army units were cannibals who slaughtered civilians. Nothing was further from the truth about our landing forces, as we were at all times instructed to show kindness to the civilians.

The airfield on Saipan was in operation, so, with the approval of the base commander, the OD sent our launch over with two officers and five of us as tourists. The officers' quest was to pick up our mail at the airfield, which had been flown in from the fleet post office at Pearl Harbor. Our quest, as enlisted personnel, was to try to find the Fourth Marine units. We had friends attached to the Third, Fourth, and Fifth Marine Divisions.

We landed at a concrete loading dock the Japanese had built but did not have time to sabotage. The officers were issued a Jeep and given directions to the airfield. We five sailors were afoot and on our own. The two gunner's mates had 1911 .45 caliber automatics; the rest of us had KA-BAR trench knives.

After bulldozing off the Japanese warehouses, the Seabees were erecting Quonset units. The Japanese had had control of Saipan for 300 years and had made quite a few improvements that had been heavily damaged by three months of air and sea bombardment.

One particular Quonset unit was almost complete, and we came upon a Marine sergeant hanging a sign above a door, which read "Square and Compass Club." Muscles and I felt obligated to be nosey and ask a few questions. When the sergeant got off the ladder, he invited us into the empty building and offered us each a bottle of warm Blatz beer. He then answered my question about the club. He and about 40 other Marines and soldiers that had made the landings were Master Masons. He further explained that the Blue Lodge of the Masonic Fraternity consisted of three classes: the apprentice degree, the fellow craft degree, and the master's degree. There are other degrees that go up to 32nd, with a final degree, 33rd (honorary). He also explained that the Blue Lodge degrees are earned by memory work; other degrees by mostly ceremony. The Scottish

Rite, the York Rite, and Shriners lodges are the others. All of these are secret fraternities and offer those who seek ancient and free enlightenment the opportunity to join.

Sergeant Brokaw explained that this island facility would be a club for Masons to gather and converse. "Our goal," he explained, "is to end this war and go home to our Mother Lodges. Of the 40 Masons in the Marine and Army units landing here, there are 30 left; 10 are buried up yonder on the hill."

Conversation over, we thanked the sergeant and caught up with the others. I told Muscles that as soon as I returned to the States—and I always felt that I would return—that I would seek out the procedure on becoming a Master Mason. (Once back in Dallas I immediately joined the Scottish Rite and am now a 32nd degree Mason.)

As we rolled into what was left of Garapan, we were really surprised to see the severity of the naval bombardment damage. We could see the results of heavy shelling from the battleships as well as troop occupation damage. Shinto shrines were all shot up from small-arms fire. The current civilian occupants were mostly Koreans, Filipinos, and a mixture of Melanesians, Micronesians, and Polynesians. The Japanese civilians believed the propaganda rhetoric about the enemy—that the U.S. forces did not take prisoners. Of course this was not true. The Japanese civilians who believed that rhetoric, mostly the women with their children, had committed suicide by jumping off the cliffs into the rocks and sea.

Time was running out, and we needed to get back to the landing to meet the mail run. We were offered a ride with a Navy Seabee whose cargo was body bags. We declined and soon hitched a ride with a Marine supply truck. Our new assignment was to complete fueling and leave for Ulithi in two days. The second night in the Saipan anchorage, we were called to general quarters. The long-range shore radar had picked up flights of bogies approaching from the south and also a flight of six from the north. The flight from the north was probably from the Iwo Jima and Chichi-jima airfields. The flights from the south were probably from the Rabaul, Truk, Rota, or Palau airfields.

The picket destroyers on outer patrol began to fire as the planes approached the island. Firing by radar with tracers is not as accurate as by sight on flying targets. The Japanese bombers were loaded with 500-pound incendiary and phosphorous bombs, dropping the phosphorous bombs first to light up the island targets. It appeared that the target was the Saipan airfield, which they had erected and which, after capture, our Seabees had repaired. For two days, we had B-24 and B-17 superfortresses flying off these strips. The bombers from the north hit the Tinian airstrips first and then moved on to Saipan.

Our cruisers, two aircraft carriers, six destroyers, our tanker (IX-127), and the *Porcupine* (IX-126) put up a good barrage. Our count was six fire crashes, two in the water and four on the island. No ships were hit. Several phosphorous bombs hit the water and sent up showers of pyrotechnic fires, like a Fourth of July fireworks display. It was a beautiful but quite deadly sight.

The Saipan airstrips were heavily damaged. However, five bulldozers and 300 Seabees had repairs completed in one day. By 9:00 AM the next morning, we weighed anchor and steamed for Ulithi (Carolines). The carriers, cruisers, and destroyers sailed for Ulithi also. It was a very fine escort for two tankers and two transports.

Chapter Twenty-Four

ULITHI

✳ ✳ ✳

UPON OUR ARRIVAL AT ULITHI, our eyes beheld the largest array of ships we had ever seen: warships, carriers, transports, landing craft, tankers, minesweepers, and so on. This huge assembly was being put together for a very large invasion. The retaking of the Philippine Islands, Leyte Gulf, Samar, and Luzon was the main objective.

The saltwater grapevine told us that this campaign would probably take place in September and October of 1944. As far as the eye could see, the anchorage was filling with ships. After unloading our oil cargo to destroyers, APAs and AKAs, our orders were to return to the Marianas, rendezvous with a merchant tanker for refilling, and await further orders.

At dusk, we had no sooner anchored when we had an alert—four bogies coming in from the north, probably from Iwo

Jima and Chichi-jima. The outlying picket destroyers had picked them up on their radar. This warning gave us time to mount our guns and be ready. Of the four bogies, only three made it to Saipan. The picket destroyers had downed one. The three bogies were Val-bombers carrying 500-pound bombs instead of torpedoes. They were flying at about 12,000 feet. It looked as though their plan was to dive-bomb from that height.

There was one light carrier, two light cruisers, two Sumner Class destroyers, plus our tanker and two supply ships. Our tanker, IX-127, was camouflaged with dummy booms and winches to look like a supply vessel, supposedly a less desirable target for enemy subs and aircraft.

Two of the bogies peeled off and headed for the cruisers and carrier. All ships in the anchorage set up a heavy barrage of 20mm and 40mm AAs. The two attacking Vals were hit as they headed for the carrier. A solid steel barrage met them as they moved in from the east. The third Val passed over the airfield, destroying two Navy DC-3s. It escaped the ack-ack (an anti-aircraft, exploding at a certain altitude) and was last seen moving north toward Iwo Jima.

Both Vals shot down approaching the anchorage went down flaming about 100 yards off from the carrier *San Jacinto*. The destroyers, along with us and an APA, launched small landing lighters to search for enemy survivors. All we found was burning oil and debris, no survivors.

Japanese pilots and airmen carry no parachutes. The Vals had a pilot and one rear machine gunner with twin 7.65mm machine guns.

As usual, our black mess cooks, who manned the portside 20mm aft guns, were the first on their guns, the first to start firing, and the last to quit firing. Enough action for one day, our crew settled down and awaited our merchant tanker from Long Beach, California.

✴ ✴ ✴

NEWS FROM HOME and by the saltwater pipeline let us know that the Normandy Invasion and other landings along the French coast were progressing with heavy casualties on both sides. The Germans had moved 27 divisions to the invasion area. The Allies had landed up to 30 divisions, with 19,000 killed in action. The first 10 days, the Russians were annihilating the German Army and driving them back to the Polish border.

The Italian campaign was moving through Italy after the Anzio landings. Allied casualties were very heavy up through the Po Valley. I had high school buddies in the First, Second, Third, and Seventh Armies in Europe and also in the Fifth and Eighth Armies in Italy and through the African and Sicily campaigns.

I never knew how many made it through the war until we all gathered on the old Terry School grounds in 1946.

President Roosevelt announced that he was going to run for a fourth term, dump Henry Wallace, and have Senator Harry Truman as his running mate. Our feeling on board ship, 12,000 miles from home, was that a fourth term was too long for a sick, crippled, old man. We didn't need a king. We needed a healthy young man to get us home. President Roosevelt had led us for three years and brought us to the brink of winning this war. We felt he needed to rest. His ordeal for 12 years had been a killing schedule. My dad was a registered Democrat and a heavy union supporter. In Texas, we call this a "Yellow-dog Democrat." That is, a die-hard Democrat. The term comes from the remark that a Southerner would vote for a yellow dog before he'd vote for a Republican.

My feeling on the voting issue is that our democracy can only survive with a strong two-party system. It is important to keep in mind that as a republic, no one person runs our democracy. We vote-in Congress, senators, and other political managers at all levels of government—city, county, state, and national. Mix them up. Both parties should do their job and if they don't, it is our job to vote them out. For example, if we have a Democrat in the White House, we should have a Republican Congress and Senate, and vice versa.

I was 22 during the 1944 election, and the services did not have an absentee voting plan then. Or at least if they did, we did not hear of it. Roosevelt and Truman won the election. Henry Wallace's comment was, "The cups of inequity have been filled again." My parents would send me newspaper clippings concerning the political progress with our two-party system.

Chapter Twenty-Five

UNBECOMING CONDUCT

✳ ✳ ✳

ARLIER IN THE MONTH, we'd lost two men to "unbecoming conduct." While we were at sea, the two men
who were lovers disappeared into hold #2 forward and the
OD discovered that they were missing. The boatswain locked
them in the hold, and though they were given water they were
basically held prisoner while our OD decided what to do. On a
quick stopover at Guam, it was decided that one of the sailors,
a third class petty officer, would be taken ashore and handed
over to the naval base commander on the charge of dereliction
of duty, failure to report to muster, and actions unbecoming a
petty officer.

Sailing on to Saipan, the other sailor was put ashore with the
same charges. We later heard that they had been assigned to be
guards on some of the islands where several thousand Japanese

were still in hiding. This was considered a very dangerous assignment and for sure they would not have time for other activities.

The boatswain let the entire crew know that what sailors did on shore leave was their business, as long as they stayed out of trouble. What they did while on ship duties, however, was his business. Fueling and deck duties, as well as general quarters, required every man on task, and there could be no recreation while on the job. On this 15,000-ton, 500-foot-long ship, the extra work load created by the loss of the two sailors was certainly felt. A big ship with a crew of only 79 is spread pretty slim on normal work duties, and having lost Abdul and the two lovers, we were now 76.

During the last bogy raid, there were no personnel on their 20mm starboard, forward guns. The boatswain recruited two sailors from Saipan shore-based units to complement his deck force.

We used our time awaiting our refuel tanker to get our vessel shipshape. We restocked our 20mm ammo, cleaned sludge out of cargo tanks, updated our firefighting equipment, painted and repainted, getting ready for our next assignment.

Saipan and Tinian were well on their way to being transformed from Japanese fortifications to U.S. bases in preparation to annihilate the Japanese Empire. The airfields were expanded to double the runway lengths and widths, the heavy fortifications, and tents and barracks. In other words, we all felt, "Let's get this war over with."

In no time, the huge B-29s began to appear. The four-engine B-24s, superfortresses, P-51 fighter escorts, and B-29s had a range to hit the Japanese home islands and return (barely) to Tinian. Hence, the rumors spread that we would have to invade Iwo Jima for the emergency airfield landings.

We were closing out on 1944. By October, the reoccupying of the Philippines was being prepared. The pipeline leaked that Leyte Gulf, Samar, and Luzon would be the landing targets. The huge armadas at Ulithi, Espiritu Santo, Efate, Noumea, Saipan, and Guam would combine for this mammoth invasion. General MacArthur would be commander of all the active units, including the fleet.

The bulk of the remaining Japanese fleet was in this vicinity, Formosa, and the Philippine Sea. The date for this action was closely censored; nothing sent home by censored mail could leak this information.

Admiral Halsey commanded the Third Fleet, and J.S. McCain looked over the fast carriers group for support. In the meantime, the raids by the Japanese forces from Truk, Rota, Pelilau, and Palau on our Central Pacific forces were beginning to mount casualties.

Admiral Mitscher's carrier task forces, including Third and Fifth Fleet battleships, mounted heavy day and night raids on these remaining Japanese bastions in the Central Pacific. The result was the devastation of Truk, Rota, and Palau; and the Japanese raids on Saipan, Guam, and Tinian suddenly ceased.

Saipan had been fairly secured when we dropped anchor. A recreation area had been set up and fleet units were safe to have beach liberty; most sailors, after months of continuous sea duty with heavy enemy action on the water and in the air, welcomed it.

The kamikaze suicide attacks on our fleets were beginning to take their toll on our water-bound forces. Touching ground periodically was a must to prevent the unraveling of frayed shipboard nerves. Seeing one of these kamikazes bearing down on you has got to be one of the most frightening things a young man can witness. If you're forced to jump overboard, you're faced with five different species of sharks. And in the Central and North Pacific waters, hypothermia sets in fast. "Abandon ship" is the last order a sailor may hear.

TWO SQUADRONS OF DESTROYERS were in the anchorage. The recreation area had benches and a small stage set up for speakers. The entertainers were sailors off the anchorage group: a saxophonist, a clarinetist, two guitarists, and a drummer off the carrier. The music was fair. They went through the "Jersey Bounce," "Stardust," "Chattanooga Choo Choo," and "String of Pearls," all popular tunes.

One speaker, an officer from one of the destroyers, was actor Eddie Albert, who made a good speech on a powerful subject: "Why we are here." He told the officers who were sitting on the front-row benches to scatter because he wanted to see more enlisted men up front.

After the entertainment, we found our way to the beer shack and had a few warm ones. A boxing ring had been temporarily erected. Five-round bouts were scheduled. Boxers wore head gear and large gloves. No knockouts were planned. Carl and Sugar signed up for a round with two sailors from the cruiser *Pensacola.* Carl went into the ring first, against a 6'0" steward's mate. Carl, at 5'8", a South Dallas street fighter, couldn't reach him and had to jump up about 10 inches to make a swing. After five rounds, no blood, the referee called it a draw. Sugar, a Sugar Land and Houston street fighter, had really bloodied up his opponent by the third round of fighting. The ref closed the fight with Sugar as the winner.

Back at the ship, after fueling four destroyers and two cruisers, and with about 6,000 barrels left in our cargo tanks, we were ordered to Ulithi to empty cargo on the Seventh Fleet and await a merchant tanker from San Pedro, California, for a refill.

Chapter Twenty-Six

BATTLE STORIES

✯ ✯ ✯

ARRIVING AT ULITHI THE NEXT DAY, we immediately tied alongside the battleship ***North Carolina,*** pumped 3,000 barrels into it, and then pumped the other 3,000 barrels into transports (APAs). Ships of all calibers and sizes extended as far as the eye could see. The big invasion was drawing near. General MacArthur was in command of this battle group, and the goal was to liberate the Philippine Islands. General MacArthur said, "I will return," and there was no doubt that he would.

We would not sail with the battle fleet. Our orders were to return to Guam for the merchant tanker rendezvous. Our sister tanker, the ***Porcupine,*** loaded with a volatile cargo of 100-octane gasoline and diesel fuel totaling about 12,000 barrels, was scheduled to sail with the battle fleet.

Everything about our crew, 79 officers and enlisted men, was the same as the *Porcupine*. We were very disappointed about missing this huge invasion, but orders were orders. Returning to Guam, we began to receive news of the greatest sea battle ever fought on any ocean. By the end of October 1944, the landings on Samar and Luzon were accomplished. MacArthur had indeed returned. The landings were made without heavy resistance. The Japanese fleet command was aware of the invasion and of the huge American battle fleet on its way to the Philippine Sea and the Leyte Gulf.

We heard that Admiral Toyoda had gathered 70 warships and 750 planes, split his forces into three sections to face the U.S. Third and Seventh Fleets, which combined to total 166 warships and 1,280 planes.

We returned again to Ulithi to refuel the returning fleet of warships, transports, and supply ships. The battle-weary sailors were eager to let loose their stories of this great sea battle. Over the rails, we listened. I filled my diary, all the time listening to battle tales from the lips of these young men. Our crew was amazed at the horrors of the masses of kamikazes coming out of the sky on their suicide runs of death and destruction. We were told that our sister ship, the *Porcupine*, was hit by a kamikaze off Samar. The Val, loaded with a 500-pound bomb, hit the #3 tank at the base of the amidships house. The bomb exploded, the engine of the Val went through the bottom of the ship, ripping a huge hole below the waterline. She was going down fast. Fires had started in the #3 diesel tanks; the 100-octane tanks were aft. Most of the bridge crew was killed on impact and the rest of the crew was hitting the water. The *Porcupine* was ablaze forward.

The destroyers *Gansevoort* and *Pringle* and repair ship AGP-10 were hit and damaged by Japanese battleship shell fire 15 miles away. Although damaged, they managed to perform rescue operations and gathered survivors. Luckily, about 60 of the *Porcupine's* crew were retrieved; the other 19 died. The *Gansevoort* was ordered to torpedo the *Porcupine* before she exploded. It fired off two torpedoes; one hit the aft tanks and the *Porcupine* went down flaming, one big ball of fire.

Other supply ships—the *William Sharon* and the *John Burke*—were also hit, with the *Burke* going down with a mighty explosion. The *Sharon* was towed by the tug *Grapple* to Leyte. The *Burke's* cargo was TNT, fuel, trucks, rations, and beer bound for Leyte, now all resting on the bottom of the ocean in 200 feet of water.

Another sailor, Bill Mercer, a survivor of a destroyer (USS *Johnston*) had this story:

> As a gunner on 40mm AAs below the bridge, I heard the officers on the bridge giving the orders. The Japanese fleet was bearing down from the north. They were 16 miles to the north and firing salvos of 14- and

16-inch projectiles. We turned to port, full rudder, came in closer, and fired all 10 torpedoes. We took two hits, 14-inch projectiles hitting the bridge and the #1 gun turret. I grabbed a life jacket as the abandon ship order was given. I left my gun mount and was beside the bridge when someone above hollered, "Look out, below!" They were lowering a body down. It was an officer, as he had on khakis. His head was gone. My friend Jake was being carried to the wardroom. One of his legs was missing. Seven or eight men were preparing to abandon ship when a round hit. All of the men were blown away. Officers were yelling, "Abandon ship now!" A group of us hit the water and swam away from the ship as she was going down. We found a raft, and about 20 of us gathered around, and as many as could crawled inside. The sharks were on the move toward the area. The sailors in the water started kicking feet and thrashing. The disabled and injured began to disappear.

A Japanese destroyer steamed by within a hundred yards from our raft, which had about 20 men inside and about 10 hanging on. The Japanese sailors, many of them khaki-clad Marines, were shouting at us and waving their fists, giving us the finger as they passed. A squadron of our planes made a dive on the Japanese warship and, as much as we could make out, they too were hitting the water. Their warship was hit by several bombs.

We could see the Samar beach and began to paddle and kick, pushing our raft toward land. It appeared that a Japanese cruiser was picking up survivors from their burning destroyer. The Japanese survivors were the least of our worries at this time.

We hit the Samar landing beach before dark. We lost several men along the way. The Tenth Army and Fifth Marines were well entrenched, provided rations, and put our wounded on a hospital ship. Quite a few survivors from our destroyer and other ships were routed to an APA transport headed for Australia. Our next stop was Pearl Harbor.

OUR OFFICERS HAD BEEN CONFERRING with the alongside cruiser and destroyers. We had refueled and received good reports on the entire three battles at Leyte, Surigao, and Philippine Gulf, Samar. According to the officer's pipeline, Japan's Admiral Toyoda had split his fleet into three separate forces. Our fleet commanders had known through intelligence that the Japanese had been informed of U.S. plans for the Luzon landings through the Russian spy network. Our ally could be our enemy.

The northern Japanese force—four carriers, three without planes and one with Zekes (Zeros)—and the Singapore fleet came in through the Surigao Strait. A battleship force was detected by a U.S. submarine force, which promptly torpedoed two large Japanese cruisers and damaged a third. The next day this same Japanese battle force lost the great battleship *Musashi*, by aerial bombardment by U.S. planes.

Halsey's Third Fleet steamed north, leaving San Bernardino Strait unguarded. Admiral Kinkaid steamed south with his Seventh Fleet, and another sea battle erupted. Nishimura's Southern Fleet was literally destroyed. Admiral Oldendorf maneuvered by capping the strait and, as each Japanese warship came into view, the entire Seventh Fleet, with their heavy battleships, cruisers, and carrier planes and destroyers concentrated their 14-inch, 16-inch, 8-inch, 6-inch, and 5-inch guns on the Japanese force, wiping out all vessels except one Japanese destroyer. The next day, October 25, 1944, Admiral Kurita brought his central force, consisting of four battleships, six cruisers, and 14 destroyers, into the great sea battle. He found himself in a sea of carriers, destroyers, and destroyer escorts. Rear Admiral Sprague launched his planes from 16 U.S. carriers, along with 16 to 20 destroyers. A great battle followed. U.S. forces lost one carrier and three destroyers.

The Japanese fleet lost three cruisers and one carrier and had extensive damage to the *Yamato*, the largest battleship afloat, with 12 18-inch guns. The kamikaze suicide planes appeared in droves from the Philippine bases as well as enemy carriers.

The U.S. carriers *Santee* and *Suwannee* were hit by kamikazes; the U.S. carrier *St. Lo* was sunk after a suicide plane hit the flight deck. The ordinance aboard, torpedoes and 500-pound bombs exploded, the *St. Lo* plunged to the bottom in 500 feet of water. A lot of good men died. Before the war ended in August

1945, the kamikazes had sunk or damaged 300 ships and we had suffered 25,000 U.S. casualties.

After Halsey's Third Fleet had sunk four carriers, two cruisers, and four destroyers and damaged two large battleships, the three Japanese naval forces quit the battle.

In the meantime, General MacArthur had landed on the Philippine beach with 150,000 U.S. soldiers and Marines and was well on his way to conquering Luzon, Leyte, and Mindora and was marching on to Manila.

The Japanese desperately sent six warships and transports destined to land at Mindora. They were detected. Carrier- and land-based aircraft sank all the warships and transports. By the time the battles for the Philippines ended, the Japanese losses were 56,265 dead, with a decimated fleet leaving the seas open for our advance to the Japanese mainland.

We refueled our crippled fleet units at Ulithi and received orders to steam back to the Solomons, Purvis Bay, Espiritu Santo, and Noumea, where the remainder of the crippled U.S. Fleet units were in for repairs. The more heavily damaged units were towed or sent on their own power to Pearl Harbor.

After taking on a full load of cargo oil from a merchant tanker from Long Beach, California, we were on our way back to the Solomons, back where we had started 12 months earlier. At Espiritu Santo, we had a new cargo pump for the forward tanks installed. We fueled Third and Seventh Fleet cruisers and battleships. Four ammo supply ships replenished the warships with heavy ordinance and 40mm AA ammo. In all, the Leyte Gulf battle took a heavy toll on men, money, and materials.

I picked up a good story from a shipfitter on one of the carriers. The carrier group had lost so many Grumman Hellcat fighter planes that CINPAC had sent an urgent order to the Long Island plant for replacements. The people at Grumman responded by working 20-hour shifts and delivered 50 fighters across the country to San Francisco, where our escort carriers were waiting to load. The Japanese admiral was right. They had awakened a sleeping giant.

Chapter Twenty-Seven

NEWS FROM HOME

✳ ✳ ✳

A LETTER FROM HOME confirmed the home front war effort. Dad's Continental Gin Company, in addition to cotton gin manufacture, had been authorized by the war department to build 200-pound fragmentation bomb bodies. The whole shell was turned on their large engine lathes and routed to a plant in Birmingham, Alabama, for final assembly. TNT and detonators were then shipped to ports at San Francisco and New Orleans for further deployment. My mother wrote that her sewing factory in Dallas had 150 women working 10-hour days, 6-day weeks, sewing up khaki undershirts and shorts for the Army and white T-shirts and shorts for the Navy.

Along with the "gung ho" effort back home, there were the hoarders who, even though very patriotic, always have that old human trait to stock up for fear of a long war. A case in point was my aunt Lilly, whose husband was a supervisor for a large Dallas candy company. In addition to making hard candies for the services, they also made soft caramels for the home front. Aunt Lilly convinced my uncle to bring home a small sack of sugar every day. Before long, she had a hundred pounds of sugar stored in closets and under beds!

Well, the consequences are obvious. Ants and cockroaches by the millions converged on the house in North Dallas. My aunt and uncle had to move out. Neighbors hauled the tainted sugar outside, dug holes, and buried the remains. They moved furniture, bed clothing, and other ant-saturated household goods outside and sprayed with available insecticides. The fire department assisted by dispensing CO_2 extinguishers inside closets and other infested areas. All neighborly hands pitched in to help make the house livable again.

According to reports from home, this event was reported to the rationing board. My aunt and uncle were warned that hoarding was not criminal—however, very unpopular and un-patriotic—and that neighbors might take vigilante actions that could be harmful to their health and property. No further advice was necessary. The hoarding habit was curtailed.

My dad wrote me of another case involving the hoarding of gasoline. A friend of his at work confided to him that a neighbor was hoarding ethyl gasoline in his garage. Ethyl was a leaded additive for lower-octane gasoline to prevent pinging. This hoarder worked as a helper on a Gulf Oil Company distribution tank truck and had managed quite often to scrounge a quart of gas by draining the hoses when loading station tanks. Over a 16-month period, he managed to scrounge 100 gallons of 85-octane leaded gasoline, stored in five-gallon cans in his garage. Well, the word soon spread among his neighbors in South Dallas. The houses in that area behind Fair Park were close together, normally side by side on 50- by 150-foot lots.

A neighborhood meeting (minus one) was held, and the consensus was that the gasoline had to go. This was passed on to the neighbor who was told that he had five days to dispose of the gasoline or he would be reported to the Gulf Oil Company, as well as the war rationing board and the area fire department. Much like the good old USS *Porcupine*, one spark and the whole neighborhood would be history.

He got the message and donated his loot, five gallons at a time, to his good and loveable neighbors. Reporting him to the draft board was no threat, as he was 4F because of a leaking heart valve. Getting him fired was also no threat to him, as there were no men left to hire and most of the women were working at defense plants.

I had one aunt who was working as a switchman (lady) in the Texas and Pacific switchyards off Fitzhugh Avenue in

South Dallas. This was a very tough and menial job; however, Aunt Willie was a pretty strong lady. My uncle Harry, who had served in WWI, was also a switchman in the Downtown Dallas switchyard.

A few of us on the USS *Raccoon* conversed by censored mail with our stateside employers. Accordingly, we received mostly good news from the home front. My immediate supervisor, Tommy Kildow, married with two children, was now a manufacturing superintendent. He was still building the SNJ and AT-6 advanced training planes. This plane was probably the most produced "trainer" in history, used by both the U.S. Air Corps (AT-6) and the Navy (SNJ). They also added another plant, 500,000 square feet, and were producing main frame, wings, and tail sections for the B-24 bomber.

He informed me that Mabel, my replacement in 1942, was now a lead lady. "Super Rosie" he called her. She was supervising the punch presses and resistance spot welders. Her husband had made it through Africa, Sicily, and deep into the Italian mainland. He got a shrapnel wound at Anzio, was repaired, and back with his infantry unit. The North American plant was operating 24 hours a day, seven days a week. Just how could you lose a war with this 100% effort at home and in the battle zones?

As a result of this war, we men were a little tougher, a little sadder, and a lot wiser. We were grateful to be alive, though. The war was still in full swing, but closer to the end, with the enemy becoming desperate in suicide tactics. I'd been away a full 14 months, endured a few battles, and we'd suffered a few shrapnel hits on our ship. But we were lucky that we had not had any serious casualties. We wondered what was to come.

Chapter Twenty-Eight

CHRISTMAS 1944

✳ ✳ ✳

I N DECEMBER 1944, after leaving the Solomon Sea, we
steamed back to the Marianas, Guam, and then to Saipan,
our home base for the moment. Home papers kept us up-to-date
on the war in Europe. We were crushing the German Army. The
Italians had surrendered, the Russians were heading for Berlin,
the tyranny of the "master race" and their madman leader was
quickly coming to an end.

As the U.S. Atlantic Fleet was somewhat relieved of U-boat
pressure, warships of all classes began to transit the canal to par-
ticipate in the war with Japan. The battleships *Texas, Arkansas,*
and *Idaho,* plus six cruisers and 24 destroyers of His Majesty's
Navy were a welcome relief to our fatigued Pacific Fleet.

I overheard our executive officer, Lieutenant Moore, remark
that the British carriers were especially welcome, as they had

all-steel landing decks and the kamikazes would bounce off when doing their suicide dives. Our carriers had wooden landing decks, and Kamikazes would penetrate our ships, in many cases to the second and third decks, hitting fuel and ammunition areas. And, in several cases, as on the *Yorktown*, they made it all the way down to the engine room. The carrier *Princeton* took a 500-pound bomb that penetrated three decks, exploding the gasoline storage on the third deck. Most of the Atlantic warships were assigned to Halsey's Third Fleet, Kinkaid's Seventh Fleet, and McCain's fast carrier group. Preparations were rapidly being made for an all-out air and sea assault on the Japanese.

"Okinawa" and "Iwo Jima" were names floating across the saltwater pipelines. Our B-29 air armadas against Japan were yielding devastating Japanese losses both in airmen and aircraft. The fuel range of the B-29s from Saipan and Tinian was sufficient for the round-trip to the mainland. If there was any bad weather, winds, or flack damage, the ocean was the only landing facility left. Therefore, the acquisition of Iwo Jima for an emergency landing site was a top priority. It was a volcanic island, one mile wide and eight miles long, containing two airstrips, long enough for medium bombers. If secured, the airstrips would have to be extended about 3,000 feet to accommodate the huge B-29s.

Squadrons of B-24s and four-engine heavy bombers operating from Saipan, Guam, and Tinian made daily bombing runs on Iwo Jima. Seven battleships—the *Tennessee, Texas, Idaho, Arkansas* (just over from the Atlantic), *Pennsylvania, Maryland,* and *Mississippi*—along with cruisers and two squadrons of destroyers, made bombardment attacks on the island, hopefully rendering this pile of volcanic ash ready for invasion.

Iwo Jima was very important to the Japanese High Command, having been a Japanese possession for 300 years, along with Chichi-jima, about 200 miles to the north. CINPAC did not know what was 50 feet below the sands of this island or that the Imperial Japanese Marines (20,000 in total) would be the defenders. This force was the cream of Japan's fighting corp. There were also 5,000 Korean slave laborers, who had been there for two years building the underground fortifications, bunkers, and barracks, and storing water, food, medical, and ammo supplies.

During the invasion, the Japanese would force the Koreans out into the open to draw fire as cannon fodder. The Marines soon wised up to this and took the Koreans as prisoners. We transported 200 of these Koreans to Guam as prisoners of war. They were happy to be prisoners instead of dead cannon fodder! They bitterly hated the Japanese.

Our second Christmas on the water was approaching. December 1944 was a sad December for sailors at sea. We were safely at anchor in the Saipan anchorage, however, the bulk of the Third and Seventh Fleets were caught in a typhoon off the Philippine

Sea and suffered heavy losses in men and ships. We heard that the waves were up to 70 feet high. The weather reports were misleading and Admiral Halsey sailed his fleet into the eye of the typhoon and came under heavy criticism from the Navy's High Command. He was exempted from a court martial because of erroneous and unreliable weather reports that caused a misdirection of his fleet into the storm. Three destroyers went down with all hands lost. Seven hundred and ninety sailors drowned, no survivors. As the wave height swamped the smaller warships, water came down the stacks, exploding the boilers. The destroyers would go dead in the water and disappeared like rocks.

The heavier warships fared a little better. The cruiser *Pittsburg* had its bow wrenched off. Two carriers' decks were rolled up. British carriers that had recently joined the fleet fared much better with their steel flight decks. The pipeline reports that came in were disheartening. Fourteen ships damaged, three destroyers sunk, over a thousand lives lost—without a single shot being fired. This loss delayed fleet activity until early January 1945.

While steaming to various fueling locations from Australia, New Zealand, and the Solomon, Marshall, and Caroline island chains, we observed many battle- and weather-damaged ships. The two-foot by two-foot white crosses were appearing on many atolls and amid coconut groves throughout island outposts, and that did not include those who had died and been buried at sea.

Christmas came upon us as we were anchored at Saipan. Most of the crew attended services at a Quonset hut decorated for the Protestant's Christmas. Earlier in December, a Hanukkah service had been conducted. The Muslims did not attend any service. Most of the crew returned to the ship in the landing craft later. A few of us asked for permission to tour the now well-secured island and have Christmas dinner with the Army and Marine garrison. Permission was granted by the ship's supply officer, and four of us bummed a ride to the garrison and enjoyed a very good meal. Carl, Muscles, a fellow named Music, and I caught a Jeep to the hill village above the beach. The Navy Seabees, Army, and Marines had performed a miracle in rebuilding a devastated area, making this village livable, furnishing food and materials. I noticed the Shinto shrine had been repaired and was somewhat in order for the native worshipers. Most of the inhabitants now were Chamarros, Koreans, and Okinawans.

We moved on to Garapan and caught another Jeep patrol. We climbed to a 1,500-foot elevation overlooking our anchorage. We looked down at the numerous warships, landing craft, troop ships, and supply ships. I felt proud to think that we were standing on ground once occupied by the Imperial Japanese Marines and a prime base for the great Japanese Navy. After Midway and Leyte Gulf, we now were masters of the Central Pacific and soon, hopefully, the entire North Central Pacific.

The Marine corporal driving the Jeep drove us to the enemy burial ground. There were 4,000 bodies in a trench about 36 inches deep with volcanic ash on top. The smell was not nearly as bad as on our first visit. Our boys were buried on a flat plain under white crosses. Our driver estimated about 1,500. As we were informed at Guam, when the war was over all our dead would be moved to the National Cemetery in the Hawaiian Islands, except for those whose families requested they be returned to their home cemetery.

The corporal drove us back to the landing. We signaled our gangway watch to send a launch to pick us up. We made two trips to rendezvous island anchorages, taking on cargo oil from merchant tankers back to Guam or Saipan. There were no air raids, only distant rumbling from fleet and aircraft bombing of Rota, Truk, and Palau. Christmas had come and gone. The spirit of the occasion just wasn't the same 10,000 miles from home and family.

✳ ✳ ✳

Chapter Twenty-Nine

THE GATHERING STORM

✳ ✳ ✳

WE FOUND OUT that we had been assigned to be a part of the Iwo Jima invasion force. We were informed that this would be a heavily resisted effort by the enemy island defenders. Two-engine Betty medium bombers could make the trip from the Japanese mainland, attack our forces with 500-pound bombs, and return. No Japanese warships were expected to challenge, if reports were accurate. They only had two battleships, six cruisers, and 15 destroyers left, no carriers. Only these, plus their big "I" class submarines, were capable of offering any resistance to an invasion force such as ours, which was gathering in four anchorages. We had a very heavy force of battleships, light and heavy cruisers, numerous destroyers, several light carriers, and one of the older flat tops, the USS *Saratoga*.

We waited for favorable weather, fuel from merchant tankers (all ships were to be fully topped off), ammo supply craft, LSTs, LCIs, troop ships loaded with Marines fresh from San Diego, Army troops from the Philippines and New Guinea, and supply ships (AKAs), tugs, minesweepers, repair ships, and hospital ships. To cap off, we were almost ready.

There was some shipboard talk among the shipfitters gang. This was now my group, since I had passed my shipfitter third class rating and was now a petty officer. Awaiting final orders for the Iwo assault, idle minds among our group concocted a raid on the officers' private booze stock. Shipfitter First Class Kendall had found the officers' hiding place for booze, cold beer, eggs, special meats, and other special treats that had been gathered at various officers' clubs on various islands.

The Navy policy of no alcoholic beverages was evidently meant for enlisted personnel only. All officers on most ships in the Saipan anchorage were invited to a party at the Saipan main base club. Navy nurses off the hospital ships and shore bases would also be attending. Our chief petty officer (engine room) was assigned as OD. The gangway watch was Sugar and a seaman first class courier.

There were four of us in the shipfitters gang. I was assigned the job of skillfully removing the lock and clasp on the fridge door, as it was I who installed the latch and keeper. Carl and I attacked the fridge lock and hasp with our tools. In three minutes, we were in the box. Lo and behold, the box contained fifths of Old Fitzgerald, Old Charter, and Jack Daniels (all 90 proof); two dozen eggs; 20 pounds of lamb chops (frozen); and two cases of Acme beer. It was a full load for this small fridge.

Where the eggs came from was a mystery. A trip to New Zealand was six months behind us. The eggs could not have lasted that long. One possibility was that this loot came from one of the various merchant tankers alongside us. They were all fresh from the States and all returning to the States when they discharged their cargo. Several parties had taken place with the merchant officers over the past 18 months. Therefore, trading took place with crewmen and officers alike. We usually paid dearly for a fifth of "Old Fitz" and, at our rate of pay, couldn't afford to stock many bottles.

In any event, our goal at this time was to acquire enough booze to have a party of our own in our forward carpenter's shop by the chain lockers. Officers never visited this part of the ship. We loaded our bag with one bottle each of Old Fitz, Old Charter, and Jack Daniels Black Label; six eggs; and one case of Acme. We weren't interested in the meats. We reinstalled the latch, lock intact, made sure to leave no fingerprints, and left quietly. The heist would look like an inside job, and our party would be over, leaving no evidence.

Our four officers returned to the ship at approximately 3:00 AM. A motor launch from a nearby carrier dropped them off. Our strategy was foolproof—the perfect crime. They could not report the theft, as the Navy banned the use of alcohol aboard all Navy ships in peacetime and war.

We had boiled eggs the next morning and a cocktail party nightly for a week. None of the officers ever questioned any of the crew about the missing booze; however, there were rumblings among the officers with some finger-pointing at each other.

✳ ✳ ✳

THE NEW YEAR PASSED, and 1945 was upon us. There were to be no fireworks. This part of the Pacific was ours and fairly quiet for now. Our crew was weary, though. Sixteen months of continuous sea duty in war zones was beginning to show. I did find out that my brother-in-law, Earl Tillery, was now somewhere in New Guinea with the Twenty-Fifth Division, Thirty-Fifth Infantry, Second Battalion.

The landing forces were growing quickly. Battleships, cruisers, destroyers, and landing craft were arriving through the canal daily. The war in Europe was almost won. The price in human life was unbelievable. The number of casualties in the Pacific, if we had to invade the Japanese mainland, would be staggering. The estimated toll floating across the waters was 200,000 to

300,000 casualties. The unconditional surrender ultimatum was discussed by the president and his cabinet with plans to include Churchill and Stalin in an accord meeting upon the victory-in-Europe event.

In January 1945, the Iwo Jima and Okinawa campaign was still being planned. Transports, supply ships, and fleet battle line ships were gathering across the Central Pacific waters. The Fifth Army Air Force continuously pounded Rabaul. Mitchell B-25 medium bombers had reduced Rabaul airfields and harbor installations to rubble.

Our job, as a fleet fueling unit, was to steam to Ulithi to rendezvous with merchant tankers. We were to join other Third and Seventh Fleet fueling units, fill up, and return to Saipan for our support of the Iwo Jima invasion forces now scheduled for early February 1945. We received no further news of the Okinawa campaign.

Two squadrons of destroyers and three Coast Guard cutters had transited the canal and joined the Third Fleet warship forces. USS *Campbell,* one the older cutters, had quite a noble record in the Atlantic squadron, hounding U-boats for over three years.

The heavily loaded troopships (APAs) began to move out with supply ships (AKAs), destroyers, and cruisers. The battleships had moved out earlier in the week, probably for shore bombardments. B-24s, the four-engine Liberator bombers, were swarming out of Tinian. P-38 and P-51 fighter planes were gathering in formation for strafing assignments and also as escorts for the heavy bombers. The B-29 superbombers were flying out of Tinian daily, pounding destruction on the Japanese mainland.

The capture of Iwo Jima's two airfields was a strategic must for conducting a steady bombardment on the main island and for providing an emergency landing haven for crippled and fuel-short returning aircraft from Japan.

With full loads of cargo bunker oil, five other tankers were in anchorage. Our sister ship, the *Porcupine,* wouldn't be making this trip, since she had been sunk at Leyte. The USS *Jaguar* (IX-125) was in anchorage, carrying a half load of diesel and a half load of 100-octane aviation gas. A raid on our armada at Saipan and Guam with ammo ships—and five fully loaded tankers—would create a lot of fire and smoke. We had numerous screen destroyers at 10, 20, and 30 miles out, forming a radar perimeter for first warning and protection.

Also a new squadron of Northrop Black Widow night fighters was on steady patrol from Guam and Saipan. These new fighters were equipped with the latest long-range fighter radar and eight 50mm cannons (four on each wing) and could rid the skies of anything the Japanese could send over.

We maintained full deck watch fore and aft, armed with sawed-off Rem #12 pump shotguns with 0-0 shot. Our orders were to allow no native fishing vessel within 100 yards of the ship. There were quite a few Korean fishing boats operating out of Saipan and were considered friendly; however, they all looked alike to us. As noted, the Koreans were slave laborers used to build defenses on the islands. They became fishermen and supplied us with some nice groupers caught in the inner bays. Watching the Koreans fish was quite a show. Their small boat was used to transport about eight Koreans to an area clear of ships. Four would dive into the water and disappear to about 30-foot depth, and when a school of fish was sighted, they would pop up to the surface hollering, "Horie-dina saol." I believe that meant, "Fish over here." The other four would jump in with a net, spread the net out, and dive out of sight, coming up a few minutes later with a load of large groupers. This would go on all day until the boat was filled with fish of all species.

The problem was that a large number of enemy soldiers had escaped to the Saipan Mountains. Some were well armed and equipped with mines that could be set as magnetic mines and be attached to a ship's hull below water and triggered as a suicide detonation. Even though our hull was demagnetized with a degausser, the Japanese had found ways of attaching their mines and setting them off manually. While on watch, two sailors forward and two aft, there was a fear of seeing or hearing. At night, each watchman had a three-cell flashlight. At a sudden ripple of water or anchor chain rattle they would snap the safety off. We allowed no one near our ship unless properly identified by signal or by radio on their approach.

A few days and nights passed. Nothing exciting happened. The armadas of B-24 and B-29 heavies were constantly in and out of Tinian, Guam, and Saipan, laying waste to Truk, Rota, Rabaul, Iwo, and the Japanese mainland. One thing we didn't know until later, almost too late, was how well fortified Iwo Jima was.

The fleet began to move north, followed by LST and LCI transports loaded with the Third, Fourth, and Fifth Marine Divisions. Navy corpsmen, a Navy hospital ship, Seabee battalions, and our tankers made up the rear with minesweepers. We were a steel armada and nothing on earth or water could stop us. Our goal was to conquer a small island, one mile wide and eight miles long with two airfields we needed badly. We had been issued heavy clothing and shoes, as we were entering the cold North Pacific waters. Heavy squalls and typhoons had a habit of appearing out of nowhere. We passed two virgin volcanoes spouting steam and fire from the depths of the Jima waters. All of the upper islands are of volcanic origin, as is Iwo Jima, with an extinct volcano on the north end.

✷ ✷ ✷

Chapter Thirty

IWO JIMA

✳ ✳ ✳

A S WE PLOWED ON through the North Pacific, we
passed the time on deck. We still had a crew of 79. Our
conversations ranged from self-pity about our long term of continuous sea duty in battle zones. We hoped that, with the U.S.
closing the circle on Japan, this war should end by July 1945.
We heard of landings on Okinawa, a big island off of Honshu,
and the bulk of the Third and Seventh Fleets and fast carrier
flotillas pounding the mainland around the clock. Casualties
were heavy; kamikazes filled the skies, crashing in on destroyers, cruisers, and carriers as top-priority hits, with battleships as
second priority, because sinking a big ship was a tough kill with
a low success rate.

When we arrived at the island, we could hear heavy shell fire
and smell death. Our anchorage was designated to the north end

of Iwo, 2,000 yards off of the starboard side of Mount Suribachi, an extinct volcano. The other ships were scattered to the rear of the APA troopships. A third reserve wave of Marines was heading for the steep beaches in heavy Higgins landing craft. The battleships *Tennessee* and *Texas* were lobbing 14- and 16-inch projectiles into Mount Suribachi. We dropped anchor—60 fathoms and no bottom. The captain moved our big, heavy laden vessel with starboard anchor swinging deep, finally finding bottom at 40 fathoms (240 feet deep).

In addition to 10,000 to 12,000 barrels of oil, we had about 100 barrels of diesel and gasoline in 54-gallon drums forward and about 50 barrels of 30 wt. motor oil aft in 54-gallon drums lashed down on open decks. One spark and, adios, we would be history. After finally catching bottom, we manned our guns with rotating trips to the galley mess room.

The attack carnage continued and the smell of death, even out there on the open water, was oppressive. Day and night, we could hear the constant rattle of rifle and machine gun fire. A lot of men were dying on both sides. On our second day at anchor, the U.S. flag went up on Suribachi. About 20 Marines and Navy corpsmen were on top. The Marine commandant wanted a larger flag. A six-foot by ten-foot flag was routed to his command post from one of the LSTs. Another group found a larger pipe, made their way to the top, and planted Old Glory. Of this group, we learned that only three left the island alive—Ira Hayes, John Bradley, and Rene Gagnon. The raising of the second flag was captured in the famous photo by Joe Rosenthal.

They had begun to land trucks, Jeeps, bulldozers, and vehicles of all sizes. We finally had a barge come over from an AKA cargo ship to pick up our deck barrels of gasoline and motor oil.

A section of the beach had been leveled by bulldozers for a storage depot setup. The sea was not heavy, and we transferred our deck cargo by our booms to the heavy barge. They had six men on board and asked if we could furnish six more for helping to unload on the beach. We had six volunteers, and I was one of them. I wanted to see this hellhole of death.

As we neared the middle beach, we saw that a group of Seabees had erected a small landing dock and laid boards for rolling the barrels to the dugout pit. The stench was terrible. The Seabees told us that none of the dead, neither ours nor the Japanese, had been buried.

We had plenty of help unloading our barrels, with Marines and Seabees anxious for fuel. A Marine corporal told me that the Japanese had been well prepared for them. They had tunnels, heavily reinforced concrete bunkers, food supplies, water, underground barracks, and heavy artillery that could be hydraulically lifted and fired.

I had a steel helmet on and no weapon. I crawled out of the pit, found a shell hole and tumbled in. Small-arms fire was constant in every direction. This was real war! I peeked out the top of the shell hole and saw a scene from hell.

About 30 yards to the left, Navy nurses were treating men lying on stretchers, many of them not moving. I noticed the nurses had .45 caliber automatics strapped on their belts. This was their hospital. About 20 yards south of me were rows of body bags. There was no neutral ground as yet for a cemetery for the enemy or for our dead.

There was a Marine battalion about 50 yards ahead of my shell hole, with flame throwers spraying fire into bunker holes. What a way to die, burned alive in a concrete bunker. I slid back into my hole and was aware that I had company. Thank God my visitor was a khaki-clad Navy corpsman, PHM third class Don Yeager, who identified himself quickly. So did I.

He asked what in the hell was I doing in that shell hole? My blue Navy dungarees and shirt told him right away that I didn't belong there. I explained promptly that I was from the barge and we had just delivered barrels of motor oil, diesel, and gasoline, and that I wanted to have a closer look at this island paradise. The corpsman didn't think that was very funny and instructed me to stay low and follow him to the landing.

We went a different route to the barge landing, sliding into a large shell hole full of captured Japanese weapons no longer needed by their owners. The medic told me to take a souvenir with me. I grabbed a 6.5mm Arisaka rifle and bayonet. I also picked up a Nambu 8mm automatic pistol and stuffed it in my belt.

Returning to the barge, I found the sailors waiting for me in a big hurry to leave this island paradise. Then they noticed I had a couple of souvenirs. This prompted a no-hurry clamor as they all wanted a battlefield souvenir. The corpsman asked the coxswain if he could give them 10 minutes and he would guide five men at a time to the enemy arms cache. It was a sight to behold—10 sailors crawling through the sands of Iwo Jima, risking their lives for Japanese weapons to take home.

Sailors at sea don't experience close contact with the enemy. The enemy is usually coming out of the sky at 400 miles an hour to strafe your ship, dive-bomb, or pull a suicide dive (kamikaze). And if you're hit, all you can find are gobs of flesh, a lot of burning debris, and lots of fire. The nightmare of it all is your shipmates dying in a steel vault of burning hell. After the suicide attack, the ship's survivors begin to pull bodies out of the wreckage, fight the fires, shake off the shock, save the ship, and pray for help. The last thing that crosses a sailor's mind is looking for a souvenir. Damage-control groups evaluate damage and report to the surviving command. If the damage is uncontrollable, then abandon ship is the last recourse.

Sailors cannot dig foxholes. The cruel sea swallows you up as you hit the swells. If you survive drowning then you're confronted with the dangers of burning fuel, man-eating sharks, rescue ships rushing in and grinding up men in propellers, and, as at Leyte, Japanese warplanes strafing men foundering in the water.

As the guys returned to the barge, all had rifles or pistols. The Marines got the Japanese Samurai swords. As we approached our ship with the enemy weapons, all hell broke loose. The other 70 crewmen wanted to get their souvenirs before leaving Iwo. The captain agreed, if conditions were favorable. However, conditions never became favorable in our continuing days at Iwo Jima. We tagged and turned in our loot to the gunner's mates to be stored in our armory until further notice. We transferred fuel to four battleships, six cruisers, and 12 destroyers. One of the cruisers had survivors on board from the old carrier *Saratoga*. She had been hit by a kamikaze 50 miles off the eastern beach of Iwo.

✳ ✳ ✳

Chapter Thirty-One

THE *SARATOGA*

✶ ✶ ✶

To AUGMENT MY DIARY, I sought out a first class aviation machinist's mate survivor and received quite a story. He told me a very sad and soul-wrenching tale of abject horror and suffering by the *Saratoga's* crew.

A Japanese Val dive-bomber hit the *Saratoga's* aft deck and exploded. The 500-pound bomb and engine tore through the flight deck, hitting the plane's fuel and bombs on the second and third decks, just missing the boilers in the engine room. What was left of the engine ended up on the fourth deck.

The flight deck was extinguished, but the second, third, and fourth decks were exploding and burning quite extensively. After 12 hours of firefighting and damage control, the crew saved the ship, leaving all surviving hands fully exhausted. They had approximately 150 dead and many wounded and burned. Nearby warships transferred the wounded, moving them to Saipan and a hospital ship at Iwo Jima.

The remaining crew were ordered to bury their dead at sea and await a seagoing tug for towing aid. All ships had body bags, and the *Saratoga* had enough bags for their dead. But they didn't have any heavy ammo left to tie on the feet for sinking the bodies. They found boiler room fire bricks in the engine room and used them for weights. As they held services and slid the bodies off planks under the flag, quite a number of bricks broke the tie cords loose on the feet and the bodies floated east across the sea toward Japan. This was a sad sight to behold, said the aviation machinist's mate first class.

We were told later that when the *Saratoga* arrived in Bremerton, Washington, for repairs, the workers found another 38 bodies of sailors in a lower bunkroom burned to death. These sailors were buried on land at a national cemetery in Washington State.

We completed our fueling duties and anchored off the northwest end of Iwo. The OD passed the word at muster that we were to steam the next morning to Saipan to rendezvous with a merchant tanker for a new load and then return to Iwo to service the picket fleet, mostly destroyers. As I was not assigned a watch that night, the good night's sleep coming up was a gift from heaven.

At about 1:00 AM, all hell broke loose. General quarters sounded. We hit the deck with our life jackets in hand, heading for our guns. Our entire Texas bunch was still assigned to the five-inch .38 caliber aft deck gun. The black mess stewards had the aft 20mm AA guns, the Georgia and Brooklyn guys had the forward three-inch 50mm and 20mm AAs, and the Kansas guys had the .50 caliber machine guns on the bridge. The remainder of our crew—the Alabama, Massachusetts, and Florida guys—all had damage-control stations.

The word was passed that two squadrons of two-engine Japanese medium bombers, eight Betties, were picked up by the Marine radar on Iwo and would be over us in five minutes. We were in a total blackout mode. All of our AAs' magazines were loaded with tracers for every fifth round. Our heavy guns were set at 5,000 feet, the altitude of the Betties when they were on approach.

All of a sudden, the whole north end of Iwo was lit up with phosphorus bombs that were dropped by the first wave of Betties. The second wave began dropping their 500-pound bombs. Our batteries opened up by following the tracer fire from the destroyers, transports, and Marine beach batteries. The heavy warships had left that day for Okinawa, with picket destroyers outlying.

Our aft 20mm's were very accurate. The sky was lit up by falling, burning Betties. All of our guns had cut loose. One bomber fell blazing off our port bow, exploding and showering our old tub with smoking debris. They had dropped their bomb load from one end of the island to the other. Their targets were the Iwo airfields and Marine headquarters installations. No ships were hit.

The tally from the base ultra-sensitive radar units was that only two Betty Bombers left the area. Six had been shot down. We believed our guns had assisted in two of the crashes. We stayed on our guns until the all clear had sounded.

By the luck of the Irish, I was assigned the forward deck watch from 3:00 AM to 6:00 AM. After coffee, I trudged to the armory and picked up a 12-gauge sawed-off Remington shotgun and eight shells of 0-0 buckshot and a three-cell flashlight.

My orders from the OD were that if I saw anything crawling up our anchor chain, don't try, "Who goes there?" Use quick judgment, as the bomber that fell off our bow may have had survivors with a bad attitude toward Americans. The Marines and soldiers from Guadalcanal to Saipan learned the hard way. Japanese avoid being taken prisoner. To them, it is a disgrace to surrender; "banzai" for the emperor. For the remaining hours until daylight, all went well. A fellow named Bates rode shotgun aft and I rode shotgun forward. All we scared sailors saw were pieces of the aircraft debris floating by. No bodies, dead or alive.

A third wave of Marine reserves were launched from a nearby APA (transport) heading for the west beach landing. It was a Sunday morning. We were weighing anchor, preparing for our journey back to Saipan for a refill and then back to Iwo.

As the Higgins landing craft passed our ship, I heard the Marines singing an old favorite gospel song, "What a Friend We Have in Jesus," led by a chaplain in the front of the craft. The majority of our crew were Christian. We witnessed a few wet eyes in our crew as the last craft passed by, headed for the beach of death. As I said before, I personally always felt secure and that no harm would come to our ship. Consistently invoking the aid of the deity throughout our 24 months of battle zone duty and feeling protected by an omnipresent savior is a good feeling.

Arriving back in Saipan, awaiting our merchant tanker from Long Beach, California, Getty's Oil Fields and Refinery, we caught up on the news from that area. Our captain did schedule a beach party for our crew on Saipan with the cooks barbecuing a few slabs of mutton. Even after barbecuing over driftwood, and even with generous gobs of mustard and ketchup, it still tasted like Australian mutton. The one blessing concerning this outing: after two years of continuous sea duty in battle zones, everything—including the warm Schlitz and Pabst beer, and especially a few hours on dry land—was a great blessing.

✳ ✳ ✳

Chapter Thirty-Two

BACK TO IWO JIMA

✳ ✳ ✳

W E PICKED UP TOKYO ROSE'S BROADCAST from Japan concerning the slow and costly progress the U.S. Marines were making on Iwo Jima. "After 10 days of beach fighting, the Marines only accomplished a few yards of bloody ground on Iwo. Why, even a baby could crawl that far." She further described the successful raid by their Mitsubishi bomber planes on the island, "Our bombers completely destroyed the efforts by U.S. Marines in securing the airfield," further stating that their bombers destroyed a tanker and two cruisers.

The Rose's propaganda was not entirely correct, as we were the only tanker at Iwo during the raid and all of our cruisers and battleships had left the area two days before, steaming for Okinawa. The only damage really accomplished by the Japanese was a few craters on the airfield and two bombs on our cemetery on the east side. The boys were dead and could not be killed again. Their spirits had already returned to the God who gave them.

Quite a bit of action by Japanese submarines was taking place on the sea route from Saipan/Tinian to the Philippine Sea. The USS *Underhill*, a destroyer escort (DE), was sunk with heavy loss of life, apparently hit by a 24-inch by 10-foot "Long Lance" torpedo. This type usually cut a small warship like a DE in half. One of the crewmen, after abandoning ship, had seen a good part of his ship going down in two pieces. He later reported that 112 crewmen perished.

This brave ship, with a fighting crew, had escorted us on one of our trips through the same dangerous waters. Before arriving through the canal to the Central Pacific battle zone and joining the Third and Seventh Fleets, units saw convoy service in the Atlantic/Mediterranean off the coast of Oran, Algeria, joining the Pacific fleets in February 1945.

The destroyers and destroyer escorts suffered heavy losses performing picket patrols off Leyte, Okinawa, the Marianas, and Iwo Jima. They lost 15 vessels at Okinawa and the total lost to date in our Pacific theatre was about 50 destroyers and destroyer escorts.

Our merchant tanker, a Getty Oil Company vessel with the red, white, and black Getty colors, arrived with a load of 20,000 barrels of semi-refined bunker oil. We transferred about 12,000 barrels to our tanks and steamed back to Iwo to perform refueling duties to the eight destroyers doing picket and bird dog duties in the waters surrounding Iwo.

As we approached Iwo, the stench of death was still very much present. The large bloodsucking flies were still working the dead. As I was on radar watch in the radio room, I heard a strange language being sent to the APAs and LSTs in regard to where to land supplies and ammo. Our communications officer informed us that the message was in the Navaho language and being sent by Native American Marines to different ships. They were called Navaho code talkers. The Japanese were never able to decipher this strange language. The Indian scouts were in foxholes in different key locations, keeping our support craft informed as to the safest place to land men and supplies.

Another air raid was launched on Iwo while we were in Saipan. This time they missed the cemetery; however, they exacted heavy damage to the airfield and island personnel. We continued to fuel cruisers and destroyers from the Third and Seventh Fleets and finished unloading to APAs and AKAs. We were ordered back to Saipan for refueling and supposedly to head for Okinawa for contact with the bombardment fleet off Honshu.

The casualty report was 6,834 American dead and 19,000 enemy dead at Iwo. The odds were good—almost 3:1—but what a cost in human life!

✳ ✳ ✳

Chapter Thirty-Three

WINDING DOWN

✻ ✻ ✻

AFTER WE HAD STEAMED TO GUAM and then back to Saipan, I noticed two squadrons of destroyers anchored close to our anchorage. There were eight total, four of which had just arrived from the Atlantic Fifth Fleet. Signal lights flashed between our ship and the destroyers, to communicate arranging transfers to other ships. I questioned First Class Shipfitter Pendleton about all this signal light communication. His explanation was that James Forrestal, Secretary of the Navy, had decreed that all Navy and Marine personnel who had served 24 months of continuous sea duty in the Pacific battle zone were to be granted a 30-day leave stateside.

This order was well received by the *Raccoon's* crew; however, we felt that since the war was phasing down to the final invasion of the Japanese homelands, the chance of any of our crew being moved stateside was nil.

We received an emergency radio message that President Roosevelt had passed away at Warm Springs, Georgia. This fine old man, a great president, had worked himself to death on the job of guiding our nation to approaching sure victories in Europe and the Pacific war zone. All ships lowered flags to half-mast. There were three battleships in port. The flagship, USS *Pennsylvania*, had their band on deck playing "Hail to the Chief." The sound traveled across the bloody waters of this Pacific anchorage, bringing tears to many battle-weary eyes.

Ships arrived daily from the Atlantic Fleet. Preparations were being made for the invasion of the Japanese mainland, a dreaded operation. Estimates across the waters were that the casualty rate would be very, very high. General MacArthur was assigned as Supreme Commander. Navy, Marine, and Army forces—27 divisions—would be required.

Floating from ship to ship, island to island, the casualty estimates were that 200,000 to 300,000 men would die, 400,000 would be wounded, many ships and aircraft would go down, and that the Japanese were fully prepared for the landings. Rumors were strong and fear was great that many of us would never see our loved ones again.

Our Commander-in-Chief, Harry S. Truman, had served in World War I as an artillery captain with the AEF[6] in France. His war record was with honor. He had been a man of his word after the Potsdam Agreement with Churchill, Stalin, Eisenhower, Montgomery, and other chiefs of staff. He declared it would be the same as with Germany—unconditional surrender!

The Japanese warlords considered surrender unacceptable and vowed to defend their homeland to the last warrior. Rumors across the waters were that the Japanese were reserving their air power, suicide midget subs, and what little Navy they had left for a final, to-the-death defense.

Our huge carrier and battleship fleet, including 75 destroyers, 30 cruisers, and four squadrons on submarines, were having their day, almost drawing a full circle around the Japanese mainland from Okinawa to Honshu, with almost no resistance. A great fleet of seven battleships, along with cruiser and destroyer screens, stood 17 miles off Honshu and bombarded the great Hitachi plants almost to the ground. Not even the smokestacks were left standing.

The huge squadrons of B-29 superfortresses flying at 32,000 feet were unopposed with daily fire bombing raids. The

6   The American Expeditionary Forces or AEF was the United States military force sent to Europe in World War I that fought alongside allied forces against imperial German forces and helped the French defend the Western Front in 1918.

huge battleship *Yamato,* with four cruisers and six destroyers, made a one-way run (with only enough fuel for a one-way trip) to Okinawa to suicide-crash the U.S. fleet of carriers and other Third, Fifth, and Seventh Fleet units, as well as two British carriers and their screen units. This was a 400-mile run. They made 200 miles before being met by 396 U.S. and British aircraft. The *Yamato,* along with all cruisers and all but one destroyer, went to the bottom. Our aircraft, swarming like bees, dropped tons of bombs and torpedoes. Our losses were 10 aircraft and 8 pilots.

The next day McCain's fast carrier planes finished off the last Japanese battleship, the *Hyuga,* at Kure. No suicide planes were sent out. They would come later. The Japanese submarine fleet was still a threat and very active around the Central and North Pacific waters.

We moved our fueling operation to Tinian. Quite a few ships were moored in the shallow anchorage surrounding Tinian. We serviced transports and the heavy cruiser USS *Indianapolis,* which had just arrived from San Francisco with special crates unloaded at Tinian. Quizzing the cruiser's crew yielded no clue of what was in the crates.

Two days later, the *Indianapolis* left for the Philippines. We returned to Saipan and fueled eight destroyers, several arriving from the Atlantic Fleet. After a few days, word across the waters was that the *Indianapolis* was sunk by a Japanese "I" boat in the very waters we had steamed through two weeks earlier.

The news was heartbreaking. We had chatted across the gunnels with the crewmen and they were quite happy to be returning to Samar, as the Mindora girls were quite liberal with their favors. Two "Long Lance" torpedoes hit the starboard bow and amidships, severing the bow and almost cutting the ship in two. Four hundred sailors died quickly in the forward bunkrooms, 800 hit the water. The ship broke in two and went under in 11 minutes. Later news was that even though the *Indianapolis* was overdue at their Philippine base, no great effort was expended for rescue, as the war was phasing down. Complacency was prevalent throughout the war zone.

Finally, after four days and nights in the shark-infested waters, the bobbing heads were observed by a PBY seaplane. Word was radioed in, and four destroyers full-steamed to the area. Of the 800 who hit the water, only 375 were picked up. A few bloated bodies were retrieved, but the rest were never found. The ship's captain, Charles B. McVay III, was one of the survivors.[7]

---

7   Following the *Indianapolis'* sinking, Captain McVay was blamed for the incident. He was tried on December 3-19, 1945, by a Naval Court Martial and convicted of failing to order a zigzag course to be steered, which would have minimized the danger from submarine attack. This was part of standing naval procedures at the time. The sentence of Captain McVay was remitted in its entirety because of his excellent service record. For years he suffered mental health problems stemming from guilt and shame over the tragedy, and in 1968 he committed suicide. Captain McVay was posthumously exonerated by the United States Congress in 2000.

Chapter Thirty-Four

USS *TRIPPE*

✳ ✳ ✳

ONE MORNING THE EXECUTIVE OFFICER approached me on deck with my lead petty officer, shipfitter first class, informing me to pack my sea bag. I was being transferred to the USS *Trippe* (DD-403). I was told that I was bumping their third class shipfitter who had only six months of sea duty. My 25 months gained me a berth on the *Trippe,* as they were scheduled to return to San Diego for repairs and updating. Upon arrival in San Diego, I would be granted a 30-day leave.

Oh, boy! What a dream! I thought I'd died and was on my way to heaven. In 36 minutes I had my sea bag packed, with my Arisaka rifle broken down inside it. My Nambu automatic pistol was confiscated by the OD since we weren't allowed to take pistols into California. This was a very rare, pre-war, semi-automatic Japanese pistol, and the craftsmanship was better than average. I did not believe for a moment that this was his reason for confiscating my pistol! I knew the OD had admired my treasure, but I didn't care as I was ever so happy to be heading stateside.

I bid my buddies goodbye. My Texas buddies gave me a hug and helped me and my sea bag into the whaleboat (motor launch) and off to the *Trippe*, about 200 yards off our port side. The *Trippe's* whaleboat passed us going in the opposite direction with my replacement. I gave a quick look and wave to a young blond-haired sailor leaving a small overcrowded destroyer for a large, 12,000-ton tanker with 79 men. The *Trippe*, at 1,500 tons, had a crew of 220 men.

Coming aboard, I saluted the colors. The shipfitter first class and his eight underlings greeted me and led me to the bunkroom underneath the five-inch .38 gun turret. This accommodated about 150 sailors with a bunk 18 inches wide and 70 inches long, four tiers high. What a swap! My replacement inherited a stateroom with two bunks, two high, about the size of a twin bed. You can't win 'em all!

My duties were passed on to me quickly. During general quarters, I had the aft damage-control locker, the manning of the fire pumps and aft hoses, no gun assignment. Regular duties included the weighing and maintenance of all of the ship's CO_2 bottles (weekly) and the whaleboat maintenance. Also, other than the engine, I was responsible for all steam-powered winches aft assisting the gunner's mates in maintaining the torpedo tube mechanics and depth charge firing apparatus. However, upon arrival, the first class shipfitter informed me that our orders had changed.

We, all four destroyers, were to steam to Guam and pick up Marine replacements, transport them to Iwo Jima, and then steam toward Okinawa on bird dog patrol and possible screening patrol. Here I was, going back into the action, just when I thought I was heading for home and safety. Steaming to Guam for our Marines was quite a divergence from tanker duty. Our destroyer squadron was cruising at a hefty 35 knots, with four boilers and four superheated turbines turning four screws. The 1,500-ton greyhound of the seas made good time, picked up our Marines, and made it back to Iwo Jima in 20 hours.

The bird dog patrol was a zigzag maneuver—four destroyers in line about 400 yards diagonally apart, speed at 10 to 12 knots. The purpose was to watch for downed U.S. air crewmen from the daily raids still being conducted on the Japanese mainland. This operation was considered fairly routine for most of the seamen of the *Trippe*.

This screening duty also meant that the destroyers were to watch for approaching aircraft or Japanese sea patrols. The smaller destroyers were critical tools for detecting first sightings, as they then alerted the main fleet of what was coming and maintained as much fire as was necessary to thwart and hinder the attack.

By May 1945, 13 to 15 destroyers had been hit by kamikazes and sunk with heavy loss of life. Four battleships had been damaged, three cruisers demolished, and several carriers hit and heavily damaged. At the 12-knot search speed the *Trippe* conducted in the first few days I was on board, we did pick up airmen—four dead and six alive—in their life jackets or raft boats. All of the survivors were suffering from hypothermia.

Our captains would make no burials at sea unless it was absolutely unavoidable. The dead were to be placed in a cold storage room in body bags. The survivors were taken to our sickbays and given first-class medical attention by our ensign doctor and pharmacy mates.

As we moved closer into the battle zones, we stayed on constant general quarters, being relieved for chow and restroom trips. The head, as the restrooms were called, was a room with a long toilet board with eight holes over a steel scupper with salt water at a continuous flow about three feet from your bare bottom. The salt water moved fast underneath the holes and, at times, with heavy rolls from the sea you didn't need toilet paper.

✳ ✳ ✳

Chapter Thirty-Five

VENUS RISING

✳ ✳ ✳

O NE NIGHT IN MY BUNK I started to write a poem, a prayer you could say, and all these years later I still remember it:

The great Pacific is cold, cruel, and deep
and as the sailor awaits the coming of a new day
casting a fearful and dreaded gaze upon the Eastern sky,
Knowing the foe of the east is not asleep.

So do your duty sailor, go win your war.
Cast your burdens and fears on the One above,
Aware that His grace and love is always near.
The battle will soon be over, the skies again bright and clear.

—HARRY W. DEAL, AT SEA, 1945

It was at this time that something surreal happened to me. One night, I was on the 12:00 AM to 4:00 AM watch on the bridge and on the port side of the wheelhouse, out of my view, was a sailor by the name of Cisco. It was very quiet and even though we were moving, the night felt still. There was a little ripple action on the water and the ship was gliding along quietly. At times, even though I couldn't see him, I could hear Cisco softly whistling to himself.

The time was approximately 2:15 AM when, as I scanned the southeastern skies, a very bright light suddenly appeared in the sky. At first I thought that a Japanese ship had fired a phosphorous flare to detect our patrol, as I had seen this kind of searchlight detection effort many times—at Guadalcanal, Bougainville, and Iwo Jima. However, this bright light kept moving, rising slowly upward. Since I had never been this far in the northeast Pacific waters, my reaction, at first, was one of complete wonderment. I naively thought, "What kind of warfare is this?"

This strange object in the sky cast a glittering light on the calm ripples. As I scanned the waters, visibility was suddenly very clear as the brightness of the night sky increased. The light was so intense and strong that it made our job of surveillance much easier. Had there been any downed airmen or shipwrecked sailors, we could probably have picked out their rafts quite easily, with the naked eye, within a mile's radius of the boat.

The OD opened the wheelhouse door, aware that his two bridge lookouts were really puzzled by this phenomenon. He called Cisco over to my side and explained, "The bright object is Venus, the second planet from the Sun, moving eastward, and in a few hours it will look like any another star, but right now it is glowing and appears to be close by. As well as looking for survivors, this is a good time to keep your eyes open for Japanese subs, as they normally surface at night to charge their batteries with diesel generators. In this light you should be able to spot them easily."

The OD then shut the door and we went back to our duty. It was now 3:00 AM and my relief replacement wasn't due for another hour. I kept my watch by looking over the waters, but my gaze always returned to this bright, beautiful star. Cisco returned to his portside bridge watch. About 20 minutes after the OD shut the wheelhouse door, I felt a strange presence at my right side. As I said, Cisco had returned to his post on the other side of the boat and the OD, I knew, was inside the wheelhouse and my replacement wasn't due for some time. So anyone showing up on my right side would have to walk around me or through me. A quick turn of my head revealed the ghostly figure of a young man. I could actually see the ripple of the water through him. The apparition had no hat or helmet and appeared to be wearing a khaki uniform. A breeze had come up, but his blond hair did not move.

Quite startled to say the least, I called out in a loud voice addressing this apparition straight-on, "Who are you and what are you doing here?" Cisco had apparently heard my cry and quickly appeared rounding the circular passageway in front of the bridge, calling out, "You okay, Deal?" I was too shaken to converse. I waved and managed to respond, "Uh, I'm okay." Another quick glance to my right showed me that the apparition had already departed. It must have been present for only a few seconds. Cisco later told me that he had seen nothing. But I knew I had witnessed a very brief appearance of something other-worldly, a specter, or vision of what looked to be a man in his mid-20s, clad in khakis, so he must have been a soldier or pilot. I have always felt convinced that this appearance was not a hallucination or a saltwater bad dream, and I have never wavered in feeling that I experienced for a brief moment a glimpse of a soul passing from life to another state. Later I thought that it must have been the exact moment of a soul leaving a body, of a recent war casualty rising up, passing over, and moving on to God's heaven.

In my youth I had heard some pretty fanciful ghost stories. During my junior year of high school, our family had rented a lakeside cabin on Lawter Drive in the Big Thicket City Park area of White Rock Lake, about half a mile north of the City Beach Pool on the lake. The City of Dallas allowed lots to be leased on a 99-year contract, and cabins built were subject to city expansion modes. My uncle had a lease contract to manage and operate the Big Thicket Park area. This included renting six cabins, running a small concession stand, and managing a 10- by 75-foot pier with 10 rental rowboats. Twenty bicycles could also be rented by the hour. This was a busy concession. My job was to assist old Willie, a black maintenance handyman who lived in a park house.

Old Willie kept me, a 15-year-old gullible kid, well pumped-up with ghost stories. One of his best was "The Lady of the Lake" ghost, whom he had witnessed gliding across the lake many a moonlit night. The young lady, according to Willie, was spurned by her lover. They were engaged to be married. She was waiting at the church in her pink wedding gown; the lover never showed up. He had skipped town with another girlfriend. The young bride-to-be rented a taxi and was dropped off at Winfrey Point on White Rock Lake. She waded into the lake and drowned. According to Willie, she appears on a certain night in June, gliding across the lake in her pink gown.

Willie guided me to the spot on the bank where she walked in to her watery death. Not being too-brave a young man, I enlisted the aid of some of my South Dallas cronies and we rigged up our pallets and camped out on that spot off and on for the whole month of June. No lady of the lake appeared. Maybe our campfire scared her ghost away. The lake patrolmen, in their 1936 four-door

Chevy, would come by and greet us nightly. They had been patrolling for five years and had not seen the pink apparition.

One night old Willie visited our campsite and had another ghost story for us to digest. He described how one time he crossed a footbridge spanning an inlet to Bear Creek, close to a small park on the northeast side of the footbridge. As he was walking across and approaching the end of the bridge, he heard happy, giggling voices coming from a picnic bench in the park. There were watermelon rinds on the table, partially eaten and left there earlier in the evening.

He noted the rinds were moving and the remaining melon disappearing. He crawled off the footbridge and hid in some cattails by the bank. About 30 minutes later, the chattering stopped and all was quiet. He stayed hidden until he felt the ghostly watermelon eaters had left. He rose up and glanced at the table. There was nothing left. The rinds had disappeared. Old Willie said he made quick tracks to his cabin.

After this story, we gave up our lady of the lake watch. We also felt that old Willie left us with great doubt about ghostdom and that maybe too many dreams induced by sweet Lucy, his favorite 21-proof wine, had contributed to Willie's spirit stories.

When my relief came at 4:00 AM, I made no mention of my strange experience with the ghostly appearance on the bridge, not wanting to be thought of in the same way as we had thought of old Willie. Venus was still rising and we were still moving northwest. The early morning hours were very dark and lonely, and all I wanted to do was to return to my bunk in the crowed bunkroom, aft. However, after leaving the fresh saltwater breeze, I found the odor of 150 smelly feet and bad breath enough to make me want to stay on deck until daybreak. As I lay in my not-too-comfortable canvas bunk, I couldn't sleep and I tried to digest my experience on the bridge. As I mentioned, from an early age I have believed in guardian angels. I've always felt that in my many narrow bouts with dangerous situations, I escaped because an unseen spirit was watching over me. It seemed really strange to me that I would witness such an event, but the more I thought about it, the more I felt that I was supposed to see it and that it was my duty to share what had happened. I made notes in my diary and continued to think about this experience for the rest of my life.

Chapter Thirty-Six

END OF WAR

✻ ✻ ✻

I HAD THE BOYHOOD GOOD FORTUNE of having a great and loving mother who insisted that my sister and I go to church and Sunday school every week. Our family was Christian—not the Holy Roller types, but good ole Southern Methodists. As was normal for kids with this upbringing, I had been confirmed and had accepted Christ as Savior at an early age and was quite proud of this accomplishment all my life. I had asked Christ many times while I was serving in this war to forgive my many trespasses and to pass his loving grace over this big hunk of steel heading for harm's way in the Pacific Ocean. Though I had been in very dangerous waters many times in those 27 months, first on the old tanker—the USS *Raccoon*—and now on the destroyer the USS *Trippe,* we never took direct hits. Only shrapnel and burning debris had fallen on our decks. We were also fortunate never to lose a man in battle.

Only once when moving with other destroyers into the Japanese main seaways, continuing the zigzag search pattern off the Osaka coastline, did we run into a Japanese Zeke (Zero) squadron flying high, about 20,000 feet, heading for the main fleet off Okinawa. We fired everything we had, our 40mm flak falling short, but could not elevate to their angle. The Zero pilots were the elite of the Japanese airmen, and very few would kamikaze into suicide dives on ships.

We did once witness a dogfight between a U.S. squadron of Hellcats and Chance-Vought F4U Gullwins. We were ordered to hold our fire and to keep our eyes open for "I" boats lurking in the area, but we could not ignore the dogfight. The Zero was lighter and faster than the F4U. When a Zero came at you, all you could see was a round prop hub, usually black, and the spurting of two 20mm cannons and two 7.65mm machine guns coming out of the sky with that black prop hub and fire coming from each wing. Not a good target, as the plane was fast and thin when approaching your ship at 400 MPH. What happened is that the F4U gained altitude and got behind the Zeke, which dove straight for the water and, at about 250 feet from splashing, came up out of his dive at about 50 feet from the water. The big heavy F4U, right on his tail, could not pull up. He crashed in a great splash. As the Zero pulled out going east, we fired off our 40mms guns, but there were no hits. We steamed quickly, at 36 knots, to the splash-down. No survivors were found, only oil slicks and foam. The ocean was about 5,000 feet deep at this point and the plane had sunk with great speed.

After this devastating crash, we were ordered to continue west, and en route we witnessed a salvage tug assisting the *Hazelwood,* probably taking her to Pearl Harbor for salvage or scrap. The *Hazelwood* had suffered a direct hit from one or two kamikazes and had burned from the forward turrets to the stern. It looked as if several giants with 10,000-pound sledgehammers had spent a week demolishing this vessel, then poured 10,000 gallons of high-octane gasoline on the hulk and torched the wreck for good measure. Many good men died as a result of this attack.

We continued our goal of searching for downed pilots and crewmen, dead or alive, storing the dead bodies and taking care of the injured. The destination was Iwo Jima, where we were to transfer our survivors to a hospital ship. The dead would be buried under the sands of Iwo Jima.

AFTER ARRIVING AT IWO and discharging our cargo, I asked permission to visit the island. The fighting was mostly over. The sporadic gunfire was from clean-up squads emptying the underground bunkers and caves of stragglers. My goal was to check the cemetery. Almost 6,836 of our young men were buried under the sands, along with 19,000 enemy dead in two distant cemeteries. It was a terrible price to pay for such an ugly piece of volcanic ash. I had two buddies in the Fourth Marines and one friend in the Fifth Marines who might not have made it. I found a Marine corporal chugging through the sand going to the airfield. He gave me a lift and informed me that the burials were complete, apart from losses being delivered by the patrolling ships.

The white crosses were facing east, with the names and ranks neatly painted on each. I spent two hours walking the rows of crosses. I saw no Cauley, Stover, or Miller and felt greatly relieved that possibly Ed and my other buddies had made it. The wounded had been moved to Saipan, Guam, and Pearl Harbor. If they had been wounded earlier in the war, then perhaps they were home already. We didn't have much information about who had died while we were still on tour. We were only allowed this information once we were discharged, unless we heard by word of mouth.

Iwo Jima was fairly secure at this time. There were no large, bloodsucking flies like I had seen before, and the smell of death had been washed away with pesticides, disinfectants, and the weather. P-51s were flying strafing missions from Iwo on Japanese coastal shipping. The B-29s that were not able to make it to Saipan or Tinian were using the two airfields for emergency landings. One day, 11 B-29s had to land. Both airfields became saturated with crippled planes; accordingly, three of the last six

B-29s had to ditch along the west beach, making a belly landing in the shallows. We all manned our motor launches and headed for crew rescue. The heavy B-29s would sink within five minutes. We picked 21 airmen off wings and in the drink. I am proud to say that we rescued all. No losses.

On August 4, 1945, we received orders to return to Saipan. First, the squadron was to shell a small, craggy volcanic island about four miles off the southwest side of Iwo. During the invasion, a company of Japanese Marines had escaped by small boats to this uninhabited island, about 2,000 feet wide and a mile long. Armed with a 25mm rapid-fire cannon and quite an arsenal of small arms, they were able to fire on our transports in and out of Iwo. Our job was to bombard the rocky strip and neutralize the gun emplacement.

Our four destroyers lined up, about 100 yards apart, trained our five-inch .38 turret guns, 16 total, and our 40mm portside Bofors twins, 16 total; and we were ordered to pound the island and to leave no survivors. We pulverized the south side, swung about to the north side and unloosed our guns on the starboard batteries. We circled this craggy island like a band of Indians circling a wagon train. Their returning fire suddenly ceased.

We returned to Saipan after that baptism of fire to take on more ammo. On August 7, a patrol plane sent word that the entire island we shelled was devastated. Not a living soul was observed. I'd like to say that it made me feel good, but it didn't; it just seemed like we were doing what we had to do to end this crazy war.

While anchored off Saipan harbor, we received word that President Truman had authorized the dropping of two atom bombs on the Japanese cities of Hiroshima and Nagasaki, namely, Little Boy and Fat Man, completely destroying both cities. All ships began signaling back and forth the news. No B-29s were rising off Tinian across the bay. All was quiet on the Pacific front.

Shortly afterward, Emperor Hirohito accepted the unconditional surrender terms as decreed by the Potsdam Accord.

Our radio picked up his message to his countrymen. The message was to the point; however, the Emperor never used the word "surrender."

THE DECLARATION OF CAPITULATION
Emperor Hirohito
August 15, 1945

We, the Emperor, have ordered the Imperial Government to notify the four countries: The United States, Great Britain, China, and the Soviet Union, that we accept their joint declaration. To ensure the tranquility of the subjects of the Empire and share with all the countries of the world the joy of co-prosperity, such is the rule left us by the founder of the Empire of our illustrious Ancestors, which we have endeavored to follow. Today however, the Military situation can no longer take a favorable turn and the general tendencies of the world are not to our advantage either.

What is worse, the enemy who has recently made use of an in-human bomb, subjecting innocent people to grievous wounds and massacre. The devastation is taking on incurable proportions.

To continue the war under these conditions would not only lead to the annihilation of our Nation, but the destruction of human civilization as well.

General MacArthur was appointed commander of the occupation forces, with full authority to enforce the terms of the unconditional surrender. Ten full divisions of the Tenth Army, Fourth and Fifth Marine Divisions, Naval Battalions, and British Brigades were stationed throughout the islands of Japan. My brother-in-law, Corporal Earl Tillery, was assigned to the occupation force in Japan where he remained until 1946, when he returned to Dallas to eventually become owner of the Crystal Ice Company.

Chapter Thirty-Seven

HEADING BACK

✵ ✵ ✵

SOME ISOLATED UNITS in the Japanese islands continued fighting. Our Naval forces were reduced to just a few
destroyers, four cruisers, and a very formidable submarine force.
Word floated across the waters that the outstanding Japanese
submarine commander, Hashimoto, who sank more Allied
ships than all the other commanders combined, was leading his
squadron into Kure for surrender when the six subs behind him
radioed that they were going to seek out the American fleet and
ram their subs into them on suicide mission. He radioed back to
the commanders, "Our Emperor conceded. We lost the war. Let's
go home!" All six subs followed him into Kure and turned their
vessels over to the Allies. Many ships across the Pacific were to
remain to ferry troops and supplies into occupied Japan.

My old tanker, the *Raccoon*, was ordered to Osaka for fueling duties. Our squadron of destroyers—*Mayrant, Trippe, Wilson,* and *Stack*—were ordered to San Diego for decommissioning. We were sailing for home. Our destroyers—these little greyhounds of the oceans—were tired with tired crews. The ships had been built in the Boston and New Jersey shipyards in 1938, had fought three years in the Atlantic and then the last six months in the Pacific, and were now very ready to go home.

Thank God for his protective grace. No more killing, no more burials at sea, no more white crosses on a hundred islands dotting the Pacific. My memories of these experiences will be with me always, until the day I die.

Being chosen to be visited by the spirit of one of our young warriors passing over was a great honor to me, and a lesson that will always remind me that all who died in this costly war have passed over to another world, a safe one.

We docked in Honolulu for fuel and a well-deserved shore liberty. Then we sailed to San Diego. Our squadron sailed west, sparing no fuel, no zigzagging, full speed ahead. What a great feeling! Twenty-nine months of continuous sea duty in war zones, from Guadalcanal to Iwo Jima and the waters off Japan. We sailed into San Diego on January 1, 1946.

All crewmen were granted passes and many visited Tijuana, Mexico, and the infamous Boy's Town and other places of pleasure. My first goal was to visit a laundry and have my white uniform laundered and starched, my dress blues cleaned and pressed, and my third class shipfitters petty officer chevron sewed on. I needed to prepare my sea bag for a trip to Norman, Oklahoma, the naval gunnery training base where I was to receive my discharge.

My DD Z14 discharge was prepared. I was to receive a battleship discharge, the good conduct medal, the Asiatic Pacific medal, the American Theatre medal, and the WWII medal, two battle stars, and later on a medal for American defense for gunnery duty on shore batteries off Shell Beach, Louisiana.

Two days later, I was on a train headed north to Los Angeles, California. I would change trains and then go on to Newton, Kansas, change trains again and go on to Norman, Oklahoma. All went well until we pulled into Newton, Kansas. A blizzard was blowing and the temperature was down to 6°F. Our Pullman was detached from the steam engine, destined for the roundhouse for service until 9:00 AM the next morning. Being abandoned in an area where a blizzard had left two inches of ice and snow on the ground, a Pullman full of hungry, cold servicemen is bad enough after suffering 24 to 30 months of combat duty. We all agreed that a railroad car with no heat was the maximum insult.

We banded together—three sailors, two soldiers, and two Coast Guardsmen—and left that cold Pullman. We trudged through the icy switchyards, heading for town, about half a mile south. Newton was a railroad town that folded the boardwalks at 9:00 PM. Lights out! No restaurant or business was open. Nothing was lit up. There were only two streetlights on Main Street; otherwise, it was a ghost town.

One of the soldiers, a veteran of the Philippine campaign, noticed a light on in a large Victorian two-story house on a side street. We made our way there, opened the picket gate, noisily walked up the steps, and knocked on the screen door.

A porch light came on. The curtain was pulled aside from a small window in the door and a round, slightly wrinkled face peered out. The big blue eyes got larger. To us, this was the face of an angel. The door was opened and the face of an angel was mounted on a short, plump, motherly body. Filling the door opening were three more plump, motherly bodies behind this angel. The reaction was a quick, "My God, ladies, the Army and Navy have come to Kansas."

I explained our appearance on their porch at 9:30 PM on a cold, icy January night. The four angels listened with their mouths open. The angel filling the door opened the screen door and invited seven shivering men into their warm, heavenly Kansas castle. We cleaned our shoes and boots on the porch rug and marched into a large living room with two stuffed horsehair leather couches. A very welcome, warm fire blazed in the open fireplace. The Army sergeant spoke out as we removed our pea-coats and great coats. "This is the nearest I've been to heaven in many months."

None of us had had time to pin our battle ribbons on our uniforms; however, we were all clean, neat, and very hungry. A big pot of hot coffee was set before us. We were not bashful in filling our cups. The older lady, evidently the owner of the large house, began to explain that the kitchen smelled from the food preparation for their husbands, who worked on the 8:00 PM to 12:30 AM shift in the railroad repair shops. A question was asked when we had last had food. We explained why we had left the Pullman. The dining car was closed for lack of steam, so our last meal had been at 9:00 AM that morning.

The first lady commented that this was no way to treat our war heroes. She told us to relax and make ourselves comfortable. They retired to the kitchen and we heard a lot of noise. We knew what they were doing. In about 45 minutes, the first lady poked her head out of the kitchen door and invited us in. There was a big pot of ham hocks and lima beans, a kettle of turnip greens and turnips, and a platter of real butter and warmed-up cornbread. One lady explained that this was leftovers from lunch. The men's meal was a big pot of vegetable stew, cooking on the stove.

We cleaned the bean pot, the turnip pot, and the cornbread, plus a loaf of white bread, a pound of butter, and three pots of coffee. We weren't hogs, just hungry sailors and soldiers not used to good soul food. The first lady capped us off with a platter of oatmeal cookies.

As we prepared to leave, we all dug deep in our billfolds. We came up with $100, which we happily passed on to our Kansas angels. Their reaction was simple. "You owe us nothing; we owe you boys." We all hugged the wonderful ladies and left for the icy rail yards, leaving the $100 on the couch.

Coming in sight of our three Pullmans, we noticed a switch engine coupled to the Pullmans. That meant steam heat to the Pullmans! Our conclusion was that the first lady, whose husband was a supervisor in the roundhouse, sent word by phone of our plight. The Pullmans were warm. Our angels had come to the rescue again. How could this country lose a war with such good people behind its fighting men? It couldn't.

Chapter Thirty-Eight

HOME

⁂ ⁂ ⁂

T HE NEXT MORNING, our train headed south to Norman, Oklahoma. What beautiful country we passed through. Rolling fields of wheat and corn, oil derricks as far as the eye could see, busy people working in the fields, silos full of grain, and big, fat cattle turning grass into beef. A sleeping giant indeed!

As we arrived in Norman late that night, a bus picked up about 40 of us sailors and transported us to a barracks. The discharging procedure was fast, no fanfare, "Get them home!" There was quite a list of questions. All were to be answered "yes" or "no." "Did you have any injuries? Do you have any claims? Do you have all your issued gear?"

I had no claims or injuries. My peacoat was lost on the train. (Actually, it was the same coat that the lovely Francine had borrowed in New Orleans during my training.) My beloved diary book had also been left behind, and I had no shipfitters chevron for my dress blues. After all of those months at sea it was on the homebound trip that I managed to lose my personal belongings.

A new peacoat was issued. They could not replace the diary. I remember placing it under my pillow on the Pullman the night of the Newton trip. I hoped that the Pullman porter would have a good reading session and then return it to me, as my home address was noted inside, but this did not happen. I picked up a new pair of Navy black shoes and my dress blue blouse, sewing on the WWII yellow badge, my shipfitters chevron.

I received $300 in mustering out pay and a train ticket to Dallas Union Station. Since I had joined the VFW at Saipan, by mail, a VFW representative came by and offered me help in processing my claim. However, I had none to process.

I was quickly put on a Navy bus and dropped off at the Norman depot. At 9:45 PM, a slow-moving Southern Pacific four-car passenger train pulled in. I was on my way to Dallas. After about 15 or 20 small-town stops, we finally pulled into Dallas Union Station at around 2:00 AM.

The taxi driver helped me load my sea bag, a duffel bag, and my Japanese Arisaka rifle in the trunk. The driver asked where I got the rifle. I told him that I got it on Iwo Jima; the owner didn't need it any longer. He smiled, patted me on the shoulder, and said, "Thanks."

The taxi pulled up in front of my parent's home off Scyene
Road in South Dallas at 3:15 AM. My parents had purchased a
lot next to our one-acre leased property and had built a house.
They had just finished the house in November 1945. It had two
bedrooms, a large sleeping room/den, a living room, kitchen, and
almost-complete bathroom. Knocking on the door that early on
a Saturday morning was a very hard thing to do; however, I had
written them from San Diego giving an approximate arrival date.

The lights went on and the front door opened. There was
my dad, 64 years old, turning on the porch light. His red hair
was now silver. My mom, behind him, was gray but still a good-
looking woman. My 11-year-old sister, Betty Jo, behind her, had
grown up a lot since I had last seen her, and as always she was
smiling. A lot of hugging and loving took place in a very short
time. My last trip home had been at Christmas in 1942, just before I shipped out to Algiers Navy Base in New Orleans. Thank
God I was home with no injuries, a little wiser, a little heavier,
and four years older. It was great to see my family again.

Mom boiled up a pot of tea. We talked for a while and turned
in at about 5:00 AM. After a few hours of sleep, we talked again
until almost 2:00 PM. Dad was still working at the Continental
Gin Company. As soon as Japan had surrendered, the fragmentation bomb line shut down and the manufacture of cotton gins
was continued on a large scale.

My mother's clothing mill had also shut down after the Japanese surrender. My younger sister was in junior high school at St. Edward's. My older sister's husband's Army infantry division had been routed from the Philippines to Osaka as part of the occupation force and he still wasn't home.

At first I didn't think that readjusting to civilian life would be any problem. About 12 million U.S. veterans returning home would be in the same situation, and I thought that it would be a welcome challenge and friendly transition; it sure beat being at war. I was on the phone all day Sunday inquiring about old buddies, though it was heartbreaking. Some of the old gang didn't make it back.

Ray's sister informed me that he was buried in France. Bill was wounded at Tarawa and was in the naval hospital in Washington State. Sam was wounded at Okinawa and was in the naval hospital in San Francisco. Gus's father had died the previous month while Gus was on his way home from Germany. I called Carl's mother and found out that Carl was still on the *Raccoon* when the war ended. He was on his way to Norfolk, Virginia, after re-transiting the canal, to decommission the old tanker. Ed and Shaw were also still on board and would be home by mid-April. Carl returned to Dallas and we got together for a while. We both married and pursued our new lives. My friend Josie's husband, a P-47 pilot, was shot down over Remagen and buried in Belgium. The brother of another good pal, Hank, had his P-51 shot down over Italy and he was buried there.

Back home, adjusting to civilian life was not as easy as I thought it would be, but everyone was very friendly and made us veterans feel welcome. We all worked to fit in—getting jobs, some getting married, starting families. Shaw settled in Kansas. Ed moved to North Dallas and as soon as he settled down, joined the Prudential Insurance Company as a sales rep.

Carl returned home in late May 1946. Carl and I had had jobs promised to us at the Continental Gin Company. It was still the world's largest manufacturer of cotton gin machinery. We both signed up for 52 weeks at $20 per week veteran's bonus. This program was dubbed the "52-20-12 Club," a one-year veteran's benefit.

Hellos soon wore off. Beer drinking and nightclubbing cost a lot more than $20 a week. We both joined the work staff of the Continental Gin Company. My dad, as a supervisor, put Carl in heavy fabrication on the first floor. I was assigned as layout helper in the sheet metal department and in 1947 helped design and fabricate the world's first automatic cotton picker.

About this time I got to know the lovely and beautiful Yvonne Rivers, 17 years old and just graduated from Forest Avenue High School. Many years earlier I had met Yvonne when she was only a kid, 7 or 8 years old, as she was the younger sister of my high school buddy Lee Rivers. Who would have thought that one day we would be married? Yvonne was the only girl in a family of eight brothers, five of whom served in WWII and all of whom returned home safely. Yvonne's brother Lee arranged a date between Yvonne and me, and the rest is history. We married in April 1947 and Lee married his high school friend, Bonnie, in the same month.

In 1950, I joined a company called Geophysical Service, Inc., (G.S.I.), and I worked as a machinist basically. It went public in 1952 as Texas Instruments, Inc., and grew to be an enormous company. As G.S.I., the company had 300 employees. When I retired in 1982, T.I. had about 90,000 employees worldwide. Following WWII, the GI Bill allowed for veterans like me to go to college, and I was able to take engineering classes at SMU in Dallas and later at Rice University in Houston once I had transferred there in 1954. This enabled me to move into a management position at Texas Instruments, specializing in safety issues. After 32 years, I retired from this company.

✳ ✳ ✳

YVONNE AND I HAVE NOW BEEN MARRIED some 60 years. We have lived in most of the big cities in Texas: Dallas, Houston, Austin, and now in a little town in the Texas hill country—Marble Falls. I guess I like being in Texas. Yvonne and I are fortunate to have three children—two girls and a boy—and we sure have had a lot of fun with them. Education was important to us and all of our children have succeeded in graduating from universities. Beverly, our oldest daughter, graduated from the University of Texas in Austin; Stephen, from the University of Houston; and Suzanne, from Rice University and later from New York University for her master's degree. They have been successful in their lives and work. Like most people, our children have had ups and downs in their marriages. They continue to work hard and to strive to make a difference in the world. Beverly is a teacher in Austin, Texas, and works with special-needs children. Stephen is a businessman in Houston, Texas, involved in a variety of endeavors, including real estate and software companies. Suzanne has lived in many places (France, Italy, Israel, and California) and has specialized in the preservation of art and culture. They are all wonderful people to me.

Yvonne and I are also blessed to have four beautiful grandchildren. Our oldest granddaughter, Sarah Rivers Deal, has a Ph.D. in Sociology (the first Ph.D. that we know of in the family) and teaches at the University of Oklahoma. The other three—Erin, heading soon to college, and Chandler and Charles, still in elementary school—are much younger, but I know that through their work and endeavors they will have great things to contribute to the world.

✻ ✻ ✻

LIFE HAS BEEN A REAL UPHILL CHALLENGE since many of my WWII buddies have passed on. Carl, the last, passed in April 2001. It has been sad for me to realize they are no longer here. Living these 86 years of mine has been a wonderful and gratifying experience. I feel lucky to have had this life and this family. It was also an honor and privilege to have served this great country and, most certainly, to have been a member of the greatest generation.

I feel that today's generation of young folks is just as eager to serve their country as we were in the '40s. They're just as tough and patriotic, and they are definitely better educated. Their ways are just different. However, our advantage was obvious. We had just emerged from the Great Depression. Jobs were scarce. Survival was a daily challenge. The young folks of the '40s had a little more wear and tear, and I have no doubt that the young folks of today's generation will carry the ball and keep our country strong and healthy.

I feel that my life has been blessed over and over again. There is no rational way to explain this, but I feel that my faith has played a big part—that and sheer luck. I feel very fortunate to be able to tell my story in this memoir, *Venus Rising*, named after an event that marked my life some 64 years ago. Of course, in telling this story I have come face-to-face with timeless questions about chance, random bad luck, timing, destiny, and the role that belief and faith play in what really happens in life. I'd like to think that we all have guardian angels protecting us and that the things we do not understand are just pieces of a puzzle that fit together into a larger plan that we are only able to get small glimpses of in this lifetime.

In closing, it has been my greatest honor to share with you—my family, friends, and those who are curious to know this story—my memories of my time as a young seaman serving his country during WWII.

Photo Credits for *Venus Rising:*